Montana Farm&Ranch Life

BY DANIEL N. VICHOREK

MONTANA
GEOGRAPHIC
SERIES

NUMBER 18

MONTANA MAGAZINE
AMERICAN & WORLD GEOGRAPHIC PUBLISHING

HELENA, MONTANA

DEDICATION

This book is for my mother. She said the ranch life was too lonely.

THE PHOTOGRAPHS

There is a common perception that mankind is the ruination of the planet. "Praise ignorance," says the poet, "for what man has not encountered he has not destroyed." Accordingly, photographs of beautiful landscapes usually have no evidence of humanity. In contrast, most of the photographs in this book show agricultural landscapes, the effect of humans on the land. They are the proof that we know much that not only is not destroyed, but is enhanced.

ACKNOWLEDGMENTS

To the people whose names are in this book, and who took time to answer the questions of an uninvited dude, many thanks. Thanks also to the many keepers of the wisdom who shared it with me.

Library of Congress Cataloging-in-Publication
Vichorek, Daniel N.
  Montana farm & ranch life / by Daniel N. Vichorek.
      p.   cm. -- (Montana geographic series : no. 18)
  Includes index.
  ISBN 1-56037-016-5 : $14.95
  1. Agriculture--Montana. 2. Farm life--Montana. 3. Ranch life--Montana
  4. Farmers--Montana--Interviews. 5. Ranchers--Montana--Interviews. I.
  Title.   II. Title: Montana farm and ranch life.   III. Series.
  S451.M9V53   1992
  630'.9786--dc20   92-11558

© 1992 American & World Geographic Publishing,
P.O. Box 5630, Helena, MT 59604

Title page: Combine design near Bozeman JOHN REDDY
Front cover: Gallatin Valley wheatfield ROB OUTLAW. **Left to right:** Bill McKay winter-feeding near Roscoe MICHAEL CRUMMETT; Flathead Valley wheat harvest WAYNE MUMFORD; Ike Luke DIANE ENSIGN; Spring lambs PAUL UPDIKE. **Back cover:** top: Near East Glacier KENT & CHARLENE KRONE; **left:** Cowpuncher Craig Fillmore in the Centennial Valley TOM DIETRICH; **right:** Pickup dogs DIANE ENSIGN.

Printed in Hong Kong by Nordica International Ltd.

WAYNE MUMFORD

MICHAEL CRUMMETT

Contents

Left: *Padlock branding, Big Horn County.*
Facing page: *Combine operator.*

JEFF GNASS

Introduction

The instructions from my publisher were simple enough: "Write us a book about agriculture in Montana today. We want 30,000 words." In a way, this was like the famous instructions for capturing a polar bear: you just go up and lasso him. No instructions on what to do then.

I gave it a lot of thought. The people who know the most about agriculture, I reasoned, were farmers and ranchers. The thing to do was accost a few of these and ask them what was going on with their lives and land. I called several agricultural organizations and asked them for the names of some people who might be willing to talk. Then these people told me about some more people, and so on. From this group, I tried to select people to represent different types of agricultural operations, or operations that were similar in type but different because of their locations.

The publication *Montana Agricultural Statistics* indicates that there were approximately 25,000 farms and ranches in Montana in 1991. The sampling represented here is small, but shows the concerns and problems that cut across all aspects of agriculture. As one of my interviewees said, the politics of farmers and ranchers "go from right-right to left-left, but they all agree about some basic problems of agriculture."

Looking back on the beginnings of this book, I recall that it was my ambition to explore and clarify every aspect of agriculture in Montana. I had in mind to exhaust every topic from the operation of rod weeders to deficiency payments. In the end, it was I that was exhausted.

Consequently, this book is not encyclopedic in any way. It does not talk about all farm problems, all crops, every nuance of technology, every new inspiration for saving farming and ranching. Instead, it consists mainly of a recounting of my visits with a few agricultural producers representing diverse conditions locations and situations in Montana. It says something about the obstacles that rural people face in an increasingly urban society, and about their reasons for sticking with a job that seems thankless and has the potential to be financially ruinous. This book does not tell us much about why farmers and ranchers stay on their land. In many cases, the answer to that question is too intimate to be shared with itinerant book writers. Or maybe the question is just too stupid. They stay on their places because they are at home there.

One of the people I interviewed suggested that city people hate and envy farm and ranch people. If this is true, perhaps it is because almost nobody in the city has a home in the sense that

MICHAEL CRUMMETT

Above: Checking on a brand-new calf in the Bull Mountains.
Facing page: October in the Judith Basin country.

a farmer or rancher has a home. City people live in generic cities, each with a McDonald's and a Burger King and a Dairy Queen. We take new jobs and move a thousand miles to a city that has the same stores as the one we left. If we are diligent, we can move into a house with the same generic floorplan and the light switches in the same place as in the house we left. Farms and ranches are not generic. They share some elements, certainly, but the one that is home does not look that much like many others to the people who live there.

When I was interviewing homesteaders and their families for my previous book, *Montana's Homestead Era,* one of the people I interviewed, Oscar Guttormson, attempted to offer me some insight into his fondness for the ranch his father had homesteaded on a bleak bench south of Malta. "Sometimes when the chinook comes," he said, "I like to look off to the south. Something about the chinook makes it turn a deep purple color down there, and I like to look at it." Some years later, I chanced to be camping one night not far from Oscar's old place when the wind came up and thrashed my tent for hours until the aluminum poles were twisted into pretzels and the fabric collapsed on me. The boneless tent then whipped my inert form for the rest of the night with each mighty gust of wind. Next morning I crawled out exhausted, and facing the south, I saw a most uncanny curtain of deep blue-purple reaching from the sky to the ground. It was not a color you see in a normal life. It was some sort of outer-space, total-nuclear-war, end-of-the-world-special-effect, worst-possible-hangover purple. "Oh yeah," I said, "Oscar's purple."

I don't think I would spend my life on a place like Oscar's just for the special effects, but then, I wasn't born there.

Another failing of this book, if it is a failing, is that it does not deal with the political and environmental questions that are at the heart of agricultural concerns. The intent of this book is to acquaint non-agricultural people with the concerns of agriculture; to show, for example, how the Endangered Species Act looks to a rancher. The fact that many people hold different opinions is well-known, but an in-depth treatment of the pertinent questions is not within the scope of this book.

Given these caveats and limitations, I hope that this book nevertheless gives an accurate and sympathetic picture of agriculture in Montana today. Perhaps the reader will learn where his or her next meal will come from. As the bumper sticker says, "If you eat, you are involved in agriculture."

Daniel N. Vichorek
Helena, Montana
January 27, 1992

MICHAEL CRUMMETT

Above: Montana ram sale at Miles City.
Facing page: Southwestern Montana.

NEAL ROGERS

CHARLIE BORLAND

The Ecology of Montana Agriculture

Ecology is one of those important words that gets used a lot by people who don't have a good idea of what it means. Basically it means the overall relationship of various living things within a system. A little reflection shows that farms and ranches are a lot like living organisms themselves in some ways, and there are visible patterns in the way they relate to the big picture. This is the ecology of agriculture.

I began thinking about the ecology of farms and ranches after a conversation with Myles Watts, head of the Department of Agricultural Economics and Economics at Montana State University. "Somewhere in your book," he said, "you need to talk about the wide variation in farm and ranch units. You need to point out how the nature of the operation depends on the character of the location. Talk about the different inputs to the operations. You could mention how some small operations use a lot of workers and are heavily labor intensive, and others are land intensive, with lots of land and relatively few workers."

Right: Street corn in Huntley, 1915.
Facing page: Cornfield symmetry below the mountains.

It seems to me that Montana
ranchers and farmers fit into niches at different
scales, from local weather to international trade.

Above: *Branding on the open range, 1904.*
Facing page: *Montana Gothic, Valley County.*

I asked Dr. Watts about the role of diversification in agriculture. I was under the impression that greater diversification was one strategy for improving the farm picture. Dr. Watts said diversification tends to be overrated, partly because the operators often have difficulty adapting to farming conditions or crops that are unfamiliar to them. "We have farmers and ranchers that are very successful, and then for some reason they go to another location and fail," he said.

Something about Dr. Watts' comments made me think of mud turtles. I reflected that those displaced farmers who couldn't make it in a new place were like mud turtles taken from Swan Lake and transplanted to Big Dry Creek. The ecology was not right for them.

Two of the people I interviewed for this book, Clint Peck and Gilles Stockton, referred to the "evolution" of agriculture in Montana. "Evolution" is a word almost as interesting as ecology, and closely related to it. It means that some type of animal or plant adapts to meet existing conditions or changing conditions. One aspect of ecology is the "ecological niche." A niche consists of a specific set of conditions that meets the needs of a particular organism. A certain range of temperatures, a particular amount and pattern of precipitation, the availability of suitable forage, are a few possible elements of a niche.

It seems to me that Montana ranchers and farmers fit into niches at different scales. For example, on the local scale, each ranch and farm is tailored to local conditions. Ed Lord on Flint Creek gets one crop of grass hay, and has to be able to move his hay stacks because of heavy snowfall. In the warmer, drier country near Glendive, Dena Hoff gets three or four crops of irrigated alfalfa hay. Henry Ficken near Kalispell can raise mint, partly because he has enough water available to apply it at the rate of three inches a week all summer long. Near Alzada, Jim Courtney gets enough rain at the right time to grow dryland alfalfa and crested wheat hay.

On a larger scale, farmers and ranchers are involved in a

sort of worldwide economic ecology. A drought in Australia, Argentina, the former U.S.S.R., or Canada can have big significance for Montana wheat growers. Everybody has got to eat, as Lyndon Johnson used to say, and U.S. agricultural producers are among the big contributors to the world food supply. In fact, according to the Montana Crop and Livestock Reporting Service, American farmers, numbering fewer than three tenths of one percent of the world's farmers, produce two thirds of the world's soybeans, 46 percent of the corn, one fourth of the oranges and poultry, and 23 percent of the beef. Conventional wisdom has it that farmers and ranchers in the U.S. grow too much of everything, drive the prices down, and bring themselves to the edge of bankruptcy. The main thrust of the U.S. government's farm program is to get producers to produce less.

Agriculture is a business that involves as many decisions and as much uncertainty as any other business. Still, farmers and ranchers are different in many ways from other businessmen, and certainly different from holders of 8-to-5 jobs. As I went around interviewing agricultural people for this book, I always asked them what made them want to be farmers or ranchers. In a way it was a dumb question. Most of them probably became farmers or ranchers because it was the business they grew up with and inherited.

In another sense, the question may have been less stupid. There were certain commonalities among everybody I talked to.

Rural people like farming and ranching because they like to do hard physical work outdoors and set their own

Right and facing page: Sugar beet wagon unloading at beet dump near Laurel, 1910.

The ecology of farms and ranches is complicated not only by economics, but also by public opinion.

schedules. They like being responsible for themselves. At the end of a day they like to look back and be able to see what they did. They like to bring their children up in healthy surroundings where they can teach them the value of work and productivity. They like peace and quiet, and a slow-paced lifestyle.

They like to produce, and see things grow. It gives them joy to see healthy young animal in the spring. Al Schmitz was the only one who put many of these things into a broad perspective. He said that ranchers and farmers "maintain a moral and spiritual attitude. They are close to the mystery of life."

The ecology of farms and ranches is complicated not only by economics, but also by public opinion. Gilles Stockton said it best: "A lot of city people hate us and envy us and don't understand us." In my travels and talking to people for this book, the various consequences of misunderstanding were second only to poor crop prices in the concerns of operators.

The grounds for misunderstanding are broad. Elsewhere in this book is a section titled, "The Fate of Old Louie," wherein I discuss the differing points of view, rural versus urban, regarding animals. The awful truth is, there is no nonviolent meat. Further, there is no agriculture without some disruption of natural systems. Grazing is probably the least variation from the natural ecology of the plains, and many operators think parts of the range were in worse

Right: Four-horse binder, Gallatin County.
Facing page: Livestock prospects on homestead near Wibaux, 1910.

MONTANA HISTORICAL SOCIETY PHOTO

shape 200 years ago than they are today because of the uncontrolled grazing by buffalo.

The simple truth is, modern society has become urbanized to the point that not only are most people not farmers, but most people don't even know a farmer, or have the first clue of what goes into farming and ranching. Evidence of this is abundant whenever rural and urban people get together. For example, a rancher I know who lives far south of Malta was amazed when some hunters that he let camp on his property wanted to leave him their garbage when they left. "They were under the impression that the garbage truck would come by and get it on Wednesday," he said.

The misunderstanding between rural and urban people has deep consequences for the rural people. Perhaps the most serious has to do with the idea that agriculture lays waste to the land. No doubt there are a few farms and ranches that have been run into the ground, but these are pretty rare. The main reason is that run-down land loses its productivity and breaks the operator.

The interests of agriculture are not always going to coincide with the interests of urban people. There will always be squabbles about ranchers causing erosion, or drying up the streams. Some of these effects are unavoidable, and they leave society to choose how resources should be used. Farmers and ranchers are justifiably afraid the decision will go against them. Montana has only 25,000 farms and ranches, with 2.8 people living on each. The misunderstanding goes both ways of course. Some ranchers and farmers can't understand what would possess people to try to destroy the livelihood of the people who provide their food.

*Sheep on Powder River (**left**) and on Cinder Buttes (**facing page**).*

One place where agreement is going to be difficult between agriculture and environmentalists is in regard to endangered species.

MONTANA HISTORICAL SOCIETY PHOTO

Above: Shearing sheep and stomping wool into bags.
Facing page: This spud's for you in a Butte Chamber of Commerce competition.

Another point of contention is the use of chemicals in agricultural production. The Montana Department of Agriculture is responsible for the registration of pesticides used in Montana. As of 1991, 4,930 pesticides were registered in the state. There were 1,446 commercial and government applicators, 1,138 operators, 502 pesticide dealers, and 8,500 private applicators. Wheat farmers in Montana used $4.39 worth of chemicals per acre in 1988, according to *Montana Agricultural Statistics*. The same book shows that 5,745,000 acres of wheat were seeded in 1990, indicating that more than $25 million worth of pesticides were used on wheat alone.

The use of chemicals has become second nature for a lot of farmers and ranchers. This doesn't mean they like it. "Farmers and ranchers don't like using chemicals," Gilles Stockton said. "They always use the fewest they can." Al Schmitz has concerns about the possibility of chemicals finding their way into the food chain. Schmitz and Helen Waller both pointed out that the current government grain program requires operators to get as much production as they possibly can out of the acres they are allowed to cultivate. Both suggested that production should be limited rather than acreage, so more acres could be farmed less intensively. In this context, "less intensive" means less pesticide and chemical fertilizer. Mrs. Waller said a law to allow less intensive cropping would be "the best environmental bill they could pass." This brings to mind the comment by Gilles Stockton that "urban environmentalists are potentially the best allies we have." There are many areas of overlap between environmental concerns and agriculture. One might look forward with hope to seeing the publicity and public relations machine of the environmentalists on the side of agriculture.

One place where agreement is going to be difficult between agriculture and environmentalists is in regard to endangered species. There is no agriculture operator in Montana that doesn't tremble in his boots at the thought of what an endangered species can do to his operation. Jim

Above: Cattle on the Big Dry.
*Facing page: Pulling a grain binder with a modified
Model T Ford, Chouteau County.*

MONTANA HISTORICAL SOCIETY PHOTO

Courtney of Alzada pointed out that if a wolf were to begin harassing his livestock, he could get a year in jail and a fine of $100,000 for shooting it.

Dena Hoff fingered another sore point between ag producers and city people. "They think of us as somebody they have to subsidize with their tax money," she said. *Montana Agricultural Statistics* shows that total gross farm income in Montana in 1990 was just over $2 billion. Of this amount, $300 million was government payments. Farmers and ranchers differ in their opinions about government payments. Bill Gillin said that subsidies often are a "form of dishonesty." He told me about government payment rip-offs going clear back to the 1930s when government assistance to agriculture first became available. "It was legitimate when it started," he said. "A lot of people were hurting. But it soon turned into a racket." The problem with subsidies can be summed up easily, Bill said. "Where government money goes, corruption follows." That doesn't mean that everybody accepting a subsidy is crooked by any means, but scamsters get their chance.

The 1990 Montana Farm and Ranch Survey produced by Montana State University shows that farmers and ranchers are about evenly split on whether government price supports should be continued or dropped. About 42 percent of ranchers wanted to eliminate crop supports. Among crop producers, 47 percent wanted farm policy to continue as at present.

Right: *Bitterroot apples.*
Facing page: *Spraying chemicals on apple trees, Bitterroot Valley.*

MONTANA HISTORICAL SOCIETY PHOTO

Among ranchers who graze livestock on
public land, 67 percent oppose increases
in grazing fees.

MONTANA HISTORICAL SOCIETY PHOTO

Above: Bumper apple crop in the Bitterroot.
Facing page: Land show promotion, St. Paul, 1911.

The survey also turned up some interesting findings on
another point of contention, the use of public land by
ranchers. Among ranchers who graze livestock on public
land, 67 percent oppose increases in grazing fees. Of the
ranchers who do not use public land, 56 percent favor
grazing fee increases. The survey results do not glow with
optimism: One third of the farmers and one fifth of the
ranchers said they expect to quit within the next five years
for financial reasons.

After hearing about the various economic stresses that
afflict so many farmers and ranchers, I was glad to hear
Clint Peck's opinion that the worst of the pain may be just
about over. It was Peck who said that agriculture in Montana has evolved over the last 100 years to a point where it
is approaching long-term susceptibility on the present land
base with the present number of people. One of the major
elements in this evolution was learning to deal with the
long-term drought cycle, he said, adding that the drought
of the 1980s may have accelerated this movement. Hin-
drances to this evolution in the past have been wars that
have driven up prices and allowed the survival of some
operators who didn't have what it took to sustain operations over the long term. The fly in the ointment today, he
said, is "elitist" rich people who come to the state and buy
agricultural land that they don't use to make a living from.
If this problem doesn't upset the evolutionary progress,
Peck said, farms and ranches in Montana should get to the
point where they can survive and produce a good living for
their operators. Now, if people would only learn where food
comes from.

THE LAND OF THE
McIntosh Red.

Chamber of Commerce

BITTER ROOT VALLEY APPLES

MISSOULA MONTANA
ASK ABOUT OUR
IDEAL CLIMATE.
Summers,
Long, Cool & Delightful
Winters;
Short, Mild & Bracing.
Altitude 3225 ft.

BITTER ROOT VALLEY
APPLES.
The McIntosh Red—
bright, solid & juicy.
The Finest tasting apple
ever produced—but they said
No worms—you can eat 'em in the dark.

WESTERN
MONTANA
MISSOULA—
the Center & Gateway
to Six Rich and
Fertile Valleys:
Bitter Root
Flathead
Blackfoot
Missoula
Plains
Flint Creek
Combined Crop Acreage

Poultry, Hogs, Dairy
A million acres
awaiting you

MONTANA HISTORICAL SOCIETY PHOTO

Above: Land show, St. Paul, 1911.
Facing page: Acknowledging the corn near Billings.

The Fate of Old Loui

F arm and ranch people are not the same as city people. I speak as one who grew up on ranches in Montana, but who has lived in town and had a town job for 30 years now. The most striking difference is in the attitude of city people and rural people toward animals. This difference is so radical that trying to explain either point of view to the group holding the other point of view is a lot like explaining the strong points of the Communist party or the charitable acts of the KKK. One becomes ostracized.

This brings me to Old Louie. Old Louie is a hypothetical beef steer that I have invented for my purposes here. When I was a kid, we usually had a steer something like Old Louie fattening up in the back lot. Maybe he was the milk cow's calf, or maybe he was just some sort of cull, not good enough to sell, that we saved to eat ourselves.

Since Old Louie was around the buildings all the time, he tended to get quite tame, and sometimes would come up to the corral fence to have his ears scratched or to get fed a handful of oats by a kid. As time went on, Old Louie was seen to have his own personality that set him aside from all others of the cow kind. The fact is, as I believe, that any warm-blooded creature has a personality if you are ever in a position to discover it. Louie got to be almost like a member of the family.

Then, however, there came a certain day in the fall when it was nice and cool and there was no pressing work to do. Out came the rifle. Louie was lured into the proper position with a handful of oats and shot between the eyes. Then his throat was cut and he was hoisted up with a Farm Hand to have his guts and hide removed. The next night we would have Louie's liver for supper. No tears were shed, though we sort of missed Old Louie.

I think I was a reasonably sensitive kid, and I used to feel a little bad every time we assassinated another version of Old Louie. Still, I grew to understand that it was Old Louie's fate to be beef. Life, I could see, was not all beer and skittles. Everything on the ranch had a fate, as it turned out, even the people.

As I recall, my mother was the primary force that meted out fates on the small scale. She raised chickens that she loved dearly, but they had a specific purpose and when their time had come, she carried them gently to the chopping block, talking softly to keep them from being afraid. Then, whack whack whack, off with their heads.

Cats had a fate too. We always had a system to keep roving tomcats away from our female farm cats, but it didn't always work. Usually the chief element in the system was our dog, who somehow learned that he had a license to chase strange cats out of the country. But as I said, this system sometimes failed, and then we found ourselves with an oversupply of kittens.

My mother's rule for excess kittens was that they had to be found and knocked in the head as soon as possible. If this task could be achieved before the kittens opened their eyes and assumed personality, it would be much easier. Sometimes there would be nearly a dozen of them. I remember my mother picking them up one by one, rapping them in the head with a stick, and putting the dead ones into a bucket while the mother cat meowed pitifully. We usually let the mother cat keep one kitten for consolation, and also to keep her from being so quick to find another tomcat. Sometimes the mother cat would stash her kittens where they couldn't be reached, and the kittens would be half grown before anybody saw any of them. In that case we usually shot them one by one. Sometimes there was a reprieve from this however. My dad shot at a cat once and didn't hurt him

seriously but made a hole in his ear, which folded over like a cauliflower. The cat with the cauliflower ear was around for years because my dad said there was no double jeopardy.

I'm sure the foregoing discussion is probably distressing to some urban readers, but that's the way it is on the farm. There was no point in spaying or neutering farm cats, because they have a short life. Farm cats are stepped on by horses, run over by vehicles, eaten by coyotes, and packed off by owls, among other fates.

This attitude seems cruel and callous to city people. Yet I see far more cruelty to animals in town than on any farm or ranch. Rural people have no patience with people who are cruel or thoughtless toward animals. On the other hand, they are not overly sentimental about them either.

So much for the rural point of view. The urban view does not recognize that any animal ever dies. Old pets are not killed, they are "put to sleep." When I was working on my previous book, *Montana's Homestead Era,* I asked old timers if kids on the homesteads knew where babies came from. "Oh yes," they told me. "You watch the chickens and the bulls and the dogs and cats. You learn about sex at an early age on the farm." Nowadays, of course, everybody knows everything about sex, but nobody wants to deal with death, our own or anything else's. This aspect of the urban view was well illustrated for me by the wife of a friend of mine who could never bear to look at a whole dead chicken. When she went to the store and bought chicken, she bought disassembled parts, all of the same sort, such as all legs or all breasts. That way she didn't have to deal with the fact that a chicken had died to provide dinner.

My friend eventually got a new wife, but he was saddled with the task of trying to explain to his kids where food came from. He would take his daughters out fishing, and when they caught a fish he would show it to them and say, "See this fish? He wants to live." And then he would pick up a sap and rap the fish smartly over the head, saying, "But he can't live, because we need him for supper."

This reminds me of Albert Einstein, who was supposed

Above: *Mountain View Ranch, Fergus County.*
Facing page: *Overshot hay stacker, N-Bar Ranch, Fergus County.*

If you get too many buffalo in Yellowstone
National Park, they land in the same category
as the excessive barn cats on the ranch.

MONTANA HISTORICAL SOCIETY PHOTO

*Crow Indians branding in 1890 (**above**), and
farming (**facing page**).*

to be the smartest man in the world. He once declared the
hot dog to be a vegetable to accommodate a relative of his
who was a dedicated vegetarian but could not get over her
craving for wieners.

The perspective I am trying to impart regarding the
difference in urban and rural values explains a lot about the
current animal rights controversy. If you get too many
buffalo in Yellowstone National Park, they land in the same
category as the excessive barn cats on the ranch. Animal
rights people seem not to mind the prospect of having the
world upholstered with a profligacy of animals. I have a
strong sympathy with people who want to eliminate pain
and cruelty afflicted by humans on helpless animals, but I
don't take them too seriously unless they are rigid vegetarians who don't wear leather belts, shoes, jackets, underwear, or anything else.

Even then, you have to wonder. Recently I was complaining to a vegetarian friend of mine about the Panzer
divisions of grasshoppers that were devouring my garden.
She suggested I get some chickens to eat the hoppers. I said
that was a good idea, but then what would I do with the
chickens? "Kill them at the end of the summer," she said. I
confessed that I have become too citified to kill tame
chickens in cold blood. "Oh, just get somebody else to do
it," she said.

Ah yes. There aren't too many of us, whether we are
wearing leather underwear or buying dismembered chickens, who aren't benefiting from the raising and killing of
domestic animals. Most of us don't want to face this
unpleasantness, and so we "get somebody else to do it."
The major "somebody else" that we depend on is the
farmer and rancher.

As for me, I have more respect for the person who faces
facts, thinks about hamburger and blows the brains out of
Old Louie than for the person who neurotically buys
chicken parts. Now I see that Old Louie was lucky. He got
slaughtered by his friends.

MONTANA HISTORICAL SOCIETY PHOTO

Above: Tobacco crop west of Hamilton.
Facing page: Rounding them up on the open range, 1900.

Strategies for Surviva

Montana tends to think of itself as cattle and grain country and it mostly is, but quite a few specialty crops add variety to the scene. Other hopeful strategies such as using Montana grain to make fuel alcohol are long-term possibilities for improving the bottom line of Montana's agriculture.

SPECIALTY CROPS

The publication *Montana Agricultural Statistics* (1991) lists 18 "alternative crops" which it says are becoming increasingly important in Montana. Among them are: berseem clover, buckwheat, canola, chickling vetch, chickpeas, field peas, flax, kabocha squash, peppermint, mustard, red kidney beans, roses, safflower, soybeans and sunflowers. Some of these were grown by producers that I interviewed for this book. Rather than discuss the situation and prospects of every alternative crop or processing technology, I selected two that seem to have a significant long-term potential to transform agriculture in some areas of Montana: production and processing of safflower for diesel fuel, and production of ethane alcohol (ethanol) from grain for use in gasohol fuel.

SAFFLOWER

Safflower is an annual oilseed crop that produces several commercial products, including bird seed, feed meal for

MONTANA HISTORICAL SOCIETY PHOTO

Sorghum three miles east of Vananda.

animals, and cooking oil. In recent years, there has been a stepped-up effort to adapt safflower for use as a diesel fuel.

Research has shown that safflower oil can be used successfully to fuel medium speed diesel engines such as those used in locomotives or electric generating plants. However, high-speed diesels such as those in farm tractors have had difficulty using vegetable-based fuel because the fuel contaminates the lubricating oil, causing it to thicken. Safflower fuel also causes carbon deposits in the cylinders.

The problems with safflower can be solved. The Japanese produce a diesel engine that runs on degummed and filtered vegetable oil without problems. The trick is to produce vegetable oil that can be used as an economical fuel in existing diesel engines.

Safflower oil appears to be more economical for use as fuel than products from other Montana crops such as wheat, because it requires less energy to produce than other vegetable fuels. One gallon of diesel fuel and farm chemicals (herbicides, pesticides, fertilizer) can produce about 6.7 gallons of safflower oil.

In 1983, a national conference on vegetable fuels identified safflower as the crop closest to commercial development for producing vegetable fuel in Montana. Safflower production and refining is compatible with wheat farming. When grown in rotation with wheat, safflower can combat grassy weeds that lower grain yields. It also can be used to combat saline seep. The plant develops a tap root seven to ten feet long and uses water to a greater depth than cereal grains. The crop can be harvested with a standard grain combine. Contract prices in recent years have varied from 8 cents to 12 cents a pound, with a 2 percent price bonus for each additional 1 percent oil content.

Safflower is uniquely suited to Montana's climate, and as many as 8.5 million acres of land in Montana are considered good for growing it. Realistically, the total acreage that might be planted probably would be no more than one third of the approximately 3 million acres now planted to spring wheat. Safflower then would be grown as part of the normal crop rotation, and wheat production not substantially reduced. A typical yield per acre, 800 pounds of seed, could produce about 0.8 barrels of diesel fuel. The 800,000 barrels that could be grown on a million acres would equal about 10 percent of the diesel fuel consumed in Montana for all purposes.

Originally, safflower research in Montana was geared towards enabling farmers to use small-scale on-farm facilities to produce their own fuel from safflower they could grow themselves. It was predicted that farmers could grow enough safflower on 10 percent of their land to provide all their fuel. This scheme has been shelved, for the time being at least, and larger-scale centralized processing facilities are now foreseen.

Unfortunately, safflower is not compatible with the climate in most other states, so the interest in developing it is limited mostly to Montana. Any near-term research money to develop a usable and economical safflower fuel probably will have to come from within the state. Federal research money for renewable energy projects all but disappeared with lower and more stable petroleum prices.

Research on safflower development in Montana has been performed mostly at Montana's Eastern Agricultural Experiment Station Research Center at Sidney. More than 4,000 breeding lines of safflower have been analyzed to determine their suitability for use as fuel. Results indicate that the oil content of commercial safflower varieties can be increased from 36 percent of the seeds' weight to at least 45 percent and maybe as much as 50 percent. Part of the value of safflower is in the high protein meal by-product that can be used for animal feed. Work is needed to make this meal less bitter so it will be more palatable to livestock.

Another research goal is to reduce the cost of producing safflower oil. In 1984, safflower oil cost $2.47 a gallon. Research was aimed at reducing that cost to $1.49 by 1995. The U.S. Department of Energy has projected the cost of transportation grade diesel fuel to be about $1.50 a gallon by 1995. Proposed environmental regulations that would limit emission of some pollutants produced by burning conven-

MONTANA HISTORICAL SOCIETY PHOTO

Wheat binding gang on the Campbell Farm, Big Horn County.

The idea of using Montana grain to make
alcohol for use in gasohol
is a seductive one.

MONTANA HISTORICAL SOCIETY PHOTO

Above: Beaverslide hay stacker, Big Hole Basin.
*Facing page: The Industrial Age comes to the Great
Plains (near Havre) soon after 1900.*

tional diesel fuel could make the cleaner burning vegetable
fuel more desirable.

Research continues to make safflower a more important
crop in Montana. If economic and environmental forces also
come into play, they could for once benefit Montana
agriculture.

ETHANOL

Fuel ethanol is the same as beverage alcohol, but is
denatured by adding a small amount of gasoline or metha-
nol to make it undrinkable. The distillation process also is
the same, except it is faster and less efficient. Ten percent
ethanol is added to gasoline to make "gasohol."

Seven different ethanol manufacturing plants have
operated in Montana since 1979. As of January 1990, all of
them are out of business except for the Alcotech plant in
Ringling. New plants have been proposed for Opheim,
Hardin, Kalispell, Miles City and Great Falls.

The idea of using Montana grain to make alcohol for use
in gasohol is a seductive one. Farmers would have a new
market for grain, cattle feeders would have a new source of
high-protein food supplement from the distillers grain by-
product, and people would have cleaner air in the cities as a
result of reduced air pollution.

The only fly in the ointment is that at present, ethanol
cannot be produced at a price competitive with straight
gasoline. The present production is supported by both state
and federal subsidies, and it is not clear what will happen
when these subsidies expire. Producers' actual net costs for
producing ethanol in Montana have ranged from $1.10 to
$2.00 per gallon. The $1.10 price was the result of the federal
government providing grain from federal storage for half
price. As of 1990, Montana's net production cost was $1.43
to $1.50 per gallon.

Approximately two thirds of the gross cost of ethanol is
the purchase cost of the feedstock grain. Fluctuating grain
prices make it difficult to manufacture ethanol at a consis-
tent price. One bushel of barley yields 2.45 gallons of

ethanol, and one bushel of wheat or corn generates 2.5 gallons.

Sometimes the cost of producing ethanol can be reduced by using "distressed" grain for feedstock. An example of distressed grain is grain that has been rained on to the point that it is no longer useful for more lucrative purposes. This is not a reliable source of feedstock, however.

The major by-product of ethanol manufacture is distillers grain. In 1990, distillers grain was selling for $140 a ton, or about 44 cents per gallon of ethanol produced. This product is high-protein, 26 to 36 percent, and is sought after by dairy farmers and feedlot operators. Cattle that are fed distillers grain produce more milk and put on weight faster than if they are fed their normal feed, usually soybean or cottonseed meal.

Much of the ethanol currently produced in Montana is shipped out of state because of the higher subsidies in surrounding states. Montana ethanol distributed out of state can receive a subsidy as high as $1.30 a gallon.

Ethanol has two major hopes for expanding its use. The first is that air pollution regulations may require it to be used in areas where vehicles cause violations of the carbon monoxide standard. Great Falls, Billings and Missoula all are in violation of this standard.

The second hope is that some way can be found to manufacture ethanol more cheaply. This seems to be a serious possibility. For example, researchers in Butte have developed an enzyme that breaks grain starch into sugar without the need to heat the starch. In theory, this could reduce the cost of ethanol by at least 23 cents a gallon and perhaps as much as 38 cents a gallon. Time will tell whether a large chunk of Montana's agricultural future will run on gasohol.

Information pertaining to safflower and ethanol was provided by the Montana Department of Natural Resources and Conservation, which has funded safflower research, and by Howard Haines, DNRC's biomass engineer. ◼

MONTANA HISTORICAL SOCIETY PHOTO

Above: Cutting wheat with a header box, Hill County.
Facing page: Blackfeet agriculture class in Browning during the 1920s.

MONTANA HISTORICAL SOCIETY PHOTO

Above: Circle Diamond cattle near Hinsdale.
Facing page: Modern-day Montana cattle drive.

Money, Money, Who Got the Money?

One of the people I interviewed for this book suggested that urban people feel hate and envy for farmers and ranchers. Why would this be so? I think one reason is that city people perceive farmers as being rich, besides being free and not having to deal with all the things we deal with. Farmers and ranchers are famous for driving new cars and pickups to public meetings where they protest that they either are broke or soon will be if things don't go right for them.

The author of this book is an authority on being broke. When he is broke, he looks broke. He is not welcome in the better hotels. Conference calls are required to get approval on his credit card. Ranchers and farmers, by contrast, do not readily show their financial leanness or fatness. They look about the same whether they really are broke, or whether they have a grain bin full of large bills. "You can never tell," Clint Peck, one of my interviewees, told me. "Some of them are millionaires and they look like bums. The ones with the new cars and the new houses and equipment may well be the ones hanging on by the skin of their teeth." An old grain farmer told me, "It's okay to be broke, as long as it doesn't interfere with your lifestyle." Farmers and ranchers just get broke at a higher level than the rest of us, as probably befits people who are part of multi-million-dollar operations.

Most of the people I interviewed for this book live pretty

JOHN REDDY

low on the hog. They all have farm equipment worth more than their houses, and some of them have machines bigger than their houses.

Seeking wisdom, I fall back again on *Montana Agricultural Statistics* (1991). In this publication I learn that cash receipts by Montana farms and ranches in 1990 were $1,905,331,000. Of this, according to *Statistics*, $299,600,000 was government payments. About two thirds of the government payments were "deficiency payments." Farmers enrolled in the federal farm program receive a cash payment equal to the difference between the government's "target price" for their grain and the price the farmer actually got. It doesn't cost farmers anything to join the program, but they have to restrict the number of acres they grow, and they have to adhere to government regulations pertaining to the management of erodible land and wetland on their properties.

The Conservation Reserve Program (CRP), which pays farmers not to farm marginal land, put $108 million into Montana farmers' pockets. Wool growers got about $8 million under the Wool Act, which is financed by duties on imported wool.

One of the keys to being broke at a higher level is to sell your crops for less than they cost to grow. According to *Statistics,* Montana wheat farmers in 1988 realized a gross value of $49.89 per acre planted. However, after subtraction of all expenses, they actually wound up losing $22.34 per acre. Cattle ranchers did a little better. In 1989, Montana ranchers averaged total gross cash receipts of $387.95 per cow. After expenses, their net cash return was $19.52 per cow.

This style of being broke is financed partly by deferring some costs, such as buying new equipment, and by borrowing against equity in the farm or ranch. Sooner or later, people who do this may not be welcome in the better hotels.

So. In the meantime, who does have the money?

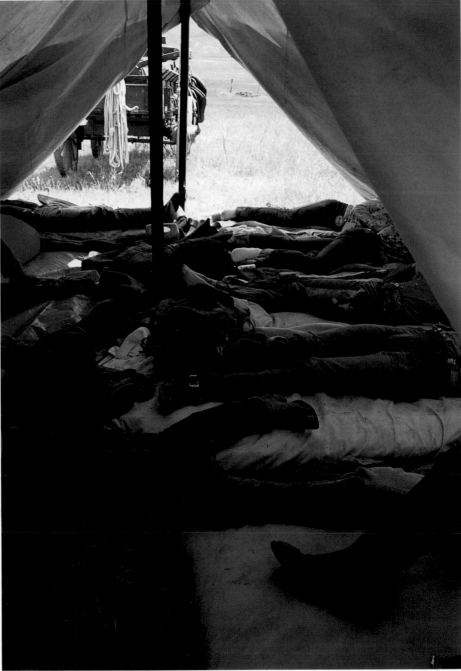

Above: Sow and piglets.
Right: Siesta time for Padlock Ranch cowboys on the Crow Indian Reservation.
Facing page: Winter team.

Agricultural True Facts, a Mystery, and a Conundrum

The Montana Crop and Livestock Reporting Service puts out a sheet titled *Agricultural Facts*. Fact number one gives rise to an agricultural conundrum. That's a question with an answer that you can never know for sure. Here we go: "Today, one farm worker produces food and fiber for 76 people. Fifty years ago, one worker only provided for 11 people."

Remarkable, a sure sign of progress and the American way. But wait a minute. Fifty years ago, that farmer did all the work himself to feed those 11 people. Nowadays, a farmer is in partnership with a bank, implement dealer, fuel supplier, fertilizer salesman, pesticide and herbicide dealer, all before he feeds or clothes a single person. After the farmer and his partners get a crop, the farmer sells it and pays his partners. New players take over the crop, process it, add to it, subtract from it, whip it this way and that, passing it though many hands until finally the product made from the farmer's crop is sold. If you add all the people who participate in these activities, it might turn out that 76 people feed one person.

Right: In the Flathead Valley.
Facing page: Sheepherder's wagon amidst a Sieben Ranch flock.

WAYNE MUMFORD

45

CONNIE WANNER

PHYLLIS LeFOHN

The conundrum is, how many people can all these people feed if they don't have the farmer?

And then the mystery, also provided in the same handout: "American agriculture is the world's largest industry with assets exceeding $1 trillion. This industry employs more than 23 million people which means that at least one out of every five people working today [in the U.S.] has an agriculturally related job—*although most of them aren't aware of it.*"

How do you work for agriculture and not know about it?

Left: Southeastern Montana.
Above: In the Absarokee Valley.
Facing page: On a Hutterite Ranch north of Harlowton.

JOHN REDDY

NEAL ROGERS

TOM DIETRICH

PATRICIA PRUITT

Above: *Center-pivot sprinkler irrigation near Horton.*
Left: *Montana is agriculture.*
Left top: *Brand-new foal.*
Facing page: *Cornfield below the Swan Range in the Flathead Valley.*

49

Profiles

DANIEL N. VICHOREK

Roger Nedens—Hardin
A LITTLE IGA OF A FARM

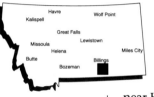

Roger Nedens is no fun in the summer. Especially not in July. When I telephoned his home near Hardin at 9 p.m. in July to ask about the possibility of an interview, he was out irrigating. "He normally gets in about 11 p.m.," his wife said.

I called at 11 p.m. and he had just gotten in. "Sure," he said, he'd be glad to talk to me if I wanted to follow him around as he worked irrigating beets. "We usually leave about five in the morning."

Sure enough, at five the next morning, he and his son Brett, 13, were ready to go. We jumped into his pickup and roared off to the beet fields. It was some time later when the first faint light of dawn began tinting the clouds in the east. By this time Roger and Brett were checking where the water had run during the night, pulling up irrigation dams, moving siphon tubes that carry water over the ditch bank and out into the beet field. I ran along behind, asking questions, taking notes and flash photographs.

I commented that coming in at 11 p.m. and getting up at five made a short night. "Yeah," Roger said, "we pretty much work our butts off five months of the year. We don't have time to go fishing but after the fall work is done there isn't much to do and everybody envies us."

Roger Nedens is in his mid-30s and has been farming on his own for 15 years. He grew up in a farming family and had no interest in punching a time clock on an eight-to-five job. He did not inherit the family farm, but managed to get into farming for himself through some share-crop arrangements, borrowing his father's equipment for the work. Today, he grows sugar beets and malting barley near Hardin, partly on his own land and partly on shares on some neighbors' land.

I asked Roger about the role of family farms in America. The family farm, he said, ain't what it used to be. "Twenty years ago," he said, "it might have been possible to raise a family on a hundred and sixty acres." No more. Today, he said, it would take at least 600 or 700 acres of his sort of farming to raise a family. This is not subsistence farming. "I'm talking raising kids and putting them through college," he said. "You can think of it in terms of a traditional family farm providing an income on par with a minimum legal wage," he said. By contrast, a larger farm could provide income comparable to a $12- to $15-an-hour job in town. "Minimum wage people don't put any kids through college," Nedens pointed out, noting that he and his wife Gayle have three children.

Roger drew a line between "the family farm" in the sense that most people think of it—"a little one-horse operation with fifty cows," as he called it—and mid-sized owner-operated farms, such as his. "A traditional little family farm trying to compete in today's market is like a mom and pop store trying to compete with Rimrock Mall in Billings. In between this little family farm and Rimrock Mall, you've got, say, your independent IGA store."

"So," I said, "you're the IGA of farming."

"I guess I'm a little IGA," he said.

At least on that limited scale, Roger said, bigger is better. On the other hand, he suggested that large-scale corporate agriculture seems to be declining in Montana. "Working for a corporation, you don't get the kind of dedication it takes to make a farm pay," he said. "You don't get people out at eleven at night and five in the morning to change the irrigating water when they're working for a corporation."

All this Roger was telling me while he and Brett worked to move their irrigation settings. The land where Roger's beets grow has been leveled, and is gone over with a "ridger," as part of the soil preparation process. The ridger makes little furrows for the water to follow down the gentle fall of the land. Each pair of furrows has its own two-inch-diameter siphon pipe delivering water from over the ditch bank. In the dirt ditches, regular plastic dams are used to stop the water and raise the level so it can be siphoned out. Some of Roger's ditches are lined with concrete in a V profile, which makes it easy to stop the water with a metal dam that exactly matches the ditch profile. Other fields are irrigated with gated pipe, which is merely a 10- or 12-inch plastic pipe that lies along the uphill side of the land and delivers water into the furrows through holes in its side. I mentioned to Roger that these methods seemed a lot easier than the sort of irrigating we did when I was a boy, trying to run water uphill on gopher-riddled mountain meadows.

"Technology makes life easier, but water doesn't run any faster than it did a hundred years ago," he said, perhaps overestimating my age.

I watched Roger's son Brett working like a man, sticking strictly to business, doing his full share of the work, and I mentioned that the boy had a totally different attitude than most kids his age. "That's one thing farming gets you," Roger said. "A kid gets the chance to be exposed to a lot of things. Most kids his age don't know anything except Nintendo. A kid working on a farm learns a lot of skills, and that can't be taken away from him."

Still, Roger noted, not every kid is suited to the farming life. One possible example is Roger's other son Chris, who doesn't share Brett's enthusiasm for getting up early in the morning. Nevertheless, even Chris is way ahead of a lot of kids. Roger mentioned, for example, that the teacher in one of Chris's classes once asked the students to "name something green," and most of the kids, living primarily in a television reality, could only think of Teenage Mutant Ninja Turtles. Chris of course was able to name all sorts of green stuff that was growing out in the field.

I suggested that Brett seemed to have already found his calling in life. "Yeah," Roger said, "I'm farming a little more land than I'd like to right now, so he can have some of it in a few years if he wants it." For his summer work, Brett gets the profits from a few acres of beets.

Roger said he thinks the future is bright for Brett and other prospective future farmers. "Land ought to get more available. The World War II generation of farmers is getting old, and somebody is going to have to take over that land. Prices for farm products are going to get better." Roger cited the situation with eastern Europe, where large populations are short of food, and predicted they will be a future market for U.S. farmers.

By the time all the irrigation water had been reset, it was mid-morning, time to go a couple miles into Hardin for breakfast. Afterwards, it was time to harvest some malt barley. Roger got into his John Deere combine, which seemed about the size of the gymnasium for a Class C school, and invited me to join him in the cab. Despite the machine's large size, it doesn't really have room for a passenger. If a passenger has a large rear end, he may not be able to avoid sitting on a switch which swings the boom around to the side, and if he continues to sit on this switch the hydraulic system will become so distressed that it will activate a piercing alarm buzzer. All this we discovered.

Nevertheless, we presently had our bin filled and dumped it into a large truck for the 50-mile run to Huntley, where the Coors brewing company has a large facility for taking in malt barley. I decided to ride the barley truck to Huntley with Roger's brother, Shawn. At the Coors plant, the truck was weighed and people working for the facility stuck long sampling tubes into the barley and got several samples which they mixed all up to determine the average quality of the barley in the load. Then they took the samples into a small room where they tested them for protein content. If barley is above 14 percent protein content, it is not suitable for brewing, and is used instead for pig feed. The price difference between malting barley and pig feed barley is three dollars per hundredweight.

Roger's barley was lower quality than it should have been because it had been damaged by hail, but it made the cut as malting barley.

After we unloaded the barley, I went into the little room where they analyzed the barley to take some pictures, but I was not happily received. I was told that there was secret information visible, and if I was going to take any pictures I would have to talk to a man who wasn't there. Having had some experience with bureaucracy and attempts to locate men who aren't there, I decided the readers of this book could do without any pictures of that particular operation.

When I called Roger in November to ask how his crops came out, I could tell that he was no longer a man trying to do ten things at once. The crops came out pretty well, he said, and he got all his beets harvested before the early freeze-up in October. He said he had a little work yet to do in the field, and some machinery to get into the shop and work on before spring.

However, he said, "Now I'm going hunting. And maybe snowmobiling. And then I'll watch some high school athletics."

MICHAEL CRUMMETT

Above: Sugar beet dumping station near Hardin.
Facing page: Roger Nedens aboard his combine.

Bill Gillin and his wife Dixie raised four children on their cattle ranch just north of Colstrip, but now their kids have grown and gone on to their own lives and Bill and Dixie are alone on the place. Bill has lived on his ranch all his life, and took the place over from his father in 1944. He sees a troubled future for agriculture.

"The trend is for big outside money to come in and buy big ranches. We don't know where the money comes from. It might be the Japanese, or drug dealers, or maybe only doctors and lawyers looking for a tax write-off. There are still good tax write-offs on agricultural land. With tax credits, it's possible to save three, four, five dollars for every dollar invested. This sort of big money investment drives the price of land up, sometimes up to three or four times the productive value." Bill said land value inflation makes it pretty much impossible for any heir to take over a ranch that has gone into estate. "A lot of these ranches that have been here for over a hundred years are going to be consolidated in the next ten to fifteen years," he said, adding, "I might be the last generation of owner-operator on this ranch."

Bill said another consequence of ranch consolidation is that small pieces of land are now rarely available for purchase by neighbors wanting to enlarge their operations. Over the years, Bill built up his holdings through purchase of a number of these small acreages. It's been a slow process, but Bill says he has five times the land now that he did when he took the place over. Further, with 40 years of effort, he managed to double the productivity of his hay land. This increase in productivity was accomplished primarily by building a system of spreader dikes to divert water from Armell's Creek and spread it over his fields.

This flooding is one of those elements in agriculture that is not to be relied upon too heavily. "Sometimes it floods three or four times in a year, sometimes it doesn't flood for three or four years."

When he was well launched into a discussion of his ranch operation, Bill suggested to me that we go out and have a look at the place, and I readily agreed. Off we went in his vintage Japanese pickup. "I've got a hundred and three thousand miles on this pickup," he said with pride. There was some rust on the body and the shock absorbers seemed a distant memory, but the little pickup served to haul a few bags of feed supplement and a weary Saint Bernard dog. We left the gravel road to follow a rough two-wheel track, and then a rougher track, and then we left off following tracks altogether and went over hill and dale looking for a bunch of cattle that Bill wanted to inspect. We broke through patches of low brush, glided through pine forests, leaped over the crest of ridges and plunged through clumps of junipers. "They gotta be around here somewhere," Bill said every once in a while, but we didn't find them.

Bill's cattle are black Angus, but he likes to use a longhorn bull for breeding his heifers, which as first-time mothers sometimes have trouble calving. The longhorn stock produces calves with small heads that are less likely to give trouble at birth. "Yeah, use that longhorn bull, and those calves come out slick and snaky," Bill said.

We continued on our rancher's tour, looking over springs and windmills, visiting horses and cows and one longhorn steer that had been retired from bull duties, observing the spreader dikes in the hayfields, and stopping for awhile at a new log cabin that some friends had recently built by a reservoir on Bill and Dixie's land.

At one point as we were checking on a stock watering tank, Bill observed the number of bullet holes shot by hooligans in the tail of his windmill and said, "They oughta pre-punch these things at the factory."

For some distance, we drove over a new road along a right of way where a fiber optic cable had been installed across the Gillin Ranch. "Things have sure changed," Bill said. He spoke approvingly of the consideration that the fiber optic company had given him in selecting the location of the cable through his ranch so as to create the fewest disturbances. This contrasted strongly with the company that had installed a natural gas line past his house and then made him wait 30 years before providing him with a connection to tap any of the gas. But then, access to public utilities and convenience is not one of the reasons one lives on a ranch. Electricity came to the Gillin Ranch in 1959, telephone service in 1969.

Ironically, it was the big coal-mining and electric-generation operations near Colstrip a few miles south that placed one of the major strains on local ranchers. "Between 1964 and 1974, taxes tripled on some ranches," Bill said.

Below: Bill Gillin.
Facing page: Near Moccasin in the Judith Basin.

DANIEL N. VICHOREK

Bill Gillin—Colstrip

FINAL GENERATION OF OWNER-OPERATOR?

A few ranches with coal on them sold out to the coal companies, but the large sums received for the land did not necessarily make life easy, Bill said. "Of the ones that sold out," he said, "half are broke and half are dead."

Things get tougher all the time for the ranchers who stay in the ranching business, Bill said. He pointed out that despite the high cattle prices in 1991, it would take three times as many calves to buy a new pickup in 1991 as in 1984. In that same period, the price of a hay swather went from 30 calves to 100 calves.

Bill is no fan of government farm subsidies. "They were okay when they first started back in the Thirties. A lot of folks were hurting then. But then it turned into a racket. None of these government programs ever do what they are intended to do. Take sodbusting, for example. They plowed up all this land so they could get govern- ment subsidies. Now they've put that same land into CRP [Conser- vation Reserve Program]. They get paid thirty or forty dollars a year per acre. I've seen a lot of that land that you could have bought for two or three dollars an acre at one time. They [CRP recipients] have a limit of fifty thousand dollars a year per operator, but we have an example right here in this county of a guy that set up dummy corporations so he could get two hundred fifty thousand dollars a year. Some of these people just have larceny in their hearts. I've been doing without these programs a hell of a long time and I'll continue. All of us ordinary farmers and ranchers would be better off without these programs. I always wonder, how do we explain these big payments to the poor taxpayer? The teacher, nurse, shopkeeper, working person who foots the bill. Some time back I was in Miles City and I saw a guy I know in a new Cadillac as long as a well rope. There had just been a story in the paper about him getting $115,000 in disaster payments, and I wondered, 'What does the poor taxpayer think?' Nothing gets done because this cheating is so widespread, so many big boys involved, that if you investi- gated it the whole program would fall apart."

DANIEL N. VICHOREK

Above: Longhorn steer from Gillin's herd.
Facing page: Along Porcupine Creek near Forsyth.

"These days, a big vacation for us is to go to Forsyth for the day."

Despite all the ups and downs over the years, Bill and Dixie look back at their ranching life with a certain amount of satisfaction. "At least we didn't have to starve any of our kids," Bill said. "That was the main thing." Not only did the Gillin kids not starve, but they apparently had quite a good time. For example, when the kids were growing up, the family took a week of vacation for camping and fishing in the Bighorn Mountains each summer. "We had a great time," Bill said.

Besides vacations in the mountains, the kids had ponies that they could ride, and all the other benefits of living on a private little kingdom. More importantly, Bill said, they learned to be self-reliant, and they learned to work. "Work is good for you," Bill said. "Show me somebody who won't work and I'll show you a worthless son-of-a-bitch."

Is there a chance that any of those self-reliant hard- working kids would want to take over the ranch and run it? Not likely. Besides the financial difficulties of inheriting the ranch, there is some doubt whether the rural lifestyle can compete these days. Bill noted, for example, that one of his sons is an airline pilot based in Colorado, where Bill's young granddaughter was taking ballet lessons. "There's no ballet lessons in Colstrip," Bill said.

So, what is going to happen to the Gillin ranch when the elder Gillins are not around to run it? "I don't know," Bill said. "We've thought about the possibility of keeping it in the family and hiring someone to run it. That way the kids could come and visit whenever they wanted to."

I asked Bill if he thought he had missed anything by spending his life on an isolated ranch. "I don't have any regrets," he said. "I'm not a fan of the opera, or winter on the Riviera. You have to adjust your wants to your abilities to provide. These days, a big vacation for us is to go to Forsyth for the day. We've got cattle and so many cats and dogs, we can't get far from home."

GEORGE WUERTHNER

TOM DIETRICH

Al Schmitz's mailing address is in Brockton, but he lives on the south side of the Missouri, right where Charlie Creek runs in. I found him there in his big house that shows signs of being whip-sawed by the elements and trampled by a whole lot of little feet. Al is the father of 14 children, whose traffic probably occasioned some of the interior wear. A hailstorm that preceded my visit by a couple of weeks took all the windows out of the west side, but Al was not too worried about this. "We'll get 'em back in before winter," he assured me. A pleasant breeze was gently stirring the curtains by the missing windows the day I was there. On the wall were the 14 large framed photographs of Al's children. His wife died in 1967, and now he shares his house with his brother Fred, a retired physicist who worked for NASA, and upon retirement returned to Charlie Creek where the stars come down to arm's length.

The windows in Al and Fred's house weren't the only hail casualties. All around the Charlie Creek country, crops were pounded flat. Al, who was 75 years old at the time of my visit and had spent nearly his whole adult life farming on Charlie Creek, said, "This was the worst hailstorm ever, around here." Of course, hailstorms are just one of the commonplace hazards a farmer faces. Al Schmitz is more interested in man-made problems that plague farmers. This interest goes way back to the days before Al was a farmer himself.

It was not foreordained that Al would be a farmer. His father, Anton, homesteaded nearby in 1910, and Al was one of nine children. He had bigger ideas than to farm. After being graduated from Sidney High School in 1934, Al went to the University of Montana in Missoula to become a lawyer. On his way to becoming a lawyer, Al took courses in economics, which got him to thinking about a question that he still asks today. The question is, "Where does money come from?"

"We studied this and that in economics, and I could never get the answer to my question," Al said. "So finally, I went up and asked the professor, 'Where does money come from?' and all he could say was, 'That's a real interesting question'."

Al never stopped thinking about this question, and a few years back he wrote a series of 15 articles which he has bound together under the title, "The Principle of Money Creation, Debt Money, The People's Burden." These articles were published in *Grass Roots,* the Farmers Union publication, and one of them appeared in the Billings *Gazette.* Other articles have been published elsewhere or turned into radio scripts.

The gist of these articles is that farmers and ranchers are producers of raw material that is essential to the creation of wealth for everybody, and therefore ought to get a reasonable return on their efforts. Instead, farmers are left out in the cold by the work of banks, big government, and big corporations.

Farmers also work against their own interests. "Farmers are so doggone independent," Al said. "They don't like to be limited." The more they produce, the lower the price, and the lower the price, the more they need to produce. "The psychology is all wrong," Al said. "You don't see General Motors producing ten times as many Chevvies as they can sell." He suggested that the price paid for farm products should be pegged to the price of things the farmer has to buy, such as tractors. This way, a given amount of grain would always have the same value as a tractor.

City people, consumers, also have the wrong idea about farmers, he said. "They think, give the farmers a raise in crop prices and it will drive the price of bread way up. The truth is that the farmer only gets six or eight cents for the wheat that is in a loaf of bread, and if you doubled what the farmer gets, it wouldn't raise the price of bread that much. On the other hand, it would double what the farmer gets for a bushel, and everybody would be better off. They'd have so much tax money coming into Helena that they'd be embarrassed not knowing what to do with it all."

The government's present farm program is faulty in many ways, Al said. One of its worst flaws is that it limits farmers in the acreage that they can plant, he said. "The program would be much better if it limited sales of grain instead of acreage, and held the extra in storage." As it is, farmers make every effort to get as much production as they can out of the acreage they are allowed. "One of the results," Al said, "is the chemicalization of our food," as a result of intensive use of pesticides, herbicides, and chemical fertilizer to maximize production.

Chemicals in the food is one of the things that concerns

Below: Al Schmitz amidst his hailed-out corn.
Facing page: Near Glendive.

DANIEL N. VICHOREK

Al Schmitz—Charlie Creek
FARMERS SEE THE MYSTERY OF LIFE

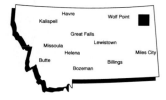

Al, whose farming is now confined to 14 acres of organic vegetables. At his peak, Al owned 2,240 acres, of which 600 were planted in grain. Al admitted he used chemicals along with everybody else, though he didn't like to.

"The herbicide goes down and affects the roots of the weeds. The trouble is, it affects other roots too. There are tons and tons of chemicals going on the land, and nobody knows just what their effects on our health may be. Some of it may come to us through our food. These are not natural chemicals, so when they enter the human body, the body doesn't know what to do with them. The body chemistry gets upset, which means the person gets sick."

It is possible to farm without chemicals, Al said, adding that nonchemical farming would be more difficult. "Farmers go to the chemicals because they want a good quick yield. Farming without chemicals takes better management, more control. One strategy for farming without chemicals is to grow a legume in rotation with grain," Al said. Sweet clover is commonly used for this purpose.

Besides growing grain and other crops, Al also ran 80 head of Hereford/ Angus–cross cattle. "We're all about half ranchers around here," he said. "Everybody has somewhere between a hundred and five hundred head of cattle along with their grain."

Besides being long on economic theory, Al places a lot of value on the philosophical elements of being a farmer. "Farmers like to produce, make things grow. They delight in seeing young things in the spring. Though they don't like to tell you about it," he said, "farmers maintain a moral and spiritual attitude. They see the mystery of life."

The values of growing are not easily given up, Al said. He pointed to the case of his brother-in-law, who lost his farm and wound up living in Oakland, California. "Now he farms his back yard."

If farm conditions don't change, Al said, individual owners are going to be driven off. "Then you'll have a rerun of what happened in the USSR." He enlarged upon this theme. "Communism means nobody is going to fix the combine with baling wire to keep it running, and nobody is going to go out in a blizzard in the middle of the night to pull a calf."

Part of our conversation took place in Al's diesel-powered Ford Escort as we rode a few miles to the site where Al's father homesteaded. The old place is deserted now, and has been for years. The original log house where Al was born is still in good shape, but the roof has started to leak. "I'll have to do something about that one of these days," Al said. In my later conversation with Al, he told me that some members of the family are looking into the possibility of having the house preserved as a historical monument.

"The barn used to be right over there," he said, gesturing at a flat spot. "Tornado got it. Got the other half of my house too," he said, indicating an abandoned frame building. "There were two halves to that house. Tornado took the south half and didn't disturb the other one. Nobody was in my house at the time. My mother and brother were in the folks' house, and they saw it go."

The tornado was in 1972. Al said they never did figure out for sure which way the tornado came from. The half of his house that was blown away went southwest. The barn appeared to go east, and a threshing machine that was parked nearby blew over to the north.

The old homestead sits at the edge of a shallow coulee that is pretty well upholstered with defunct machinery. Here are the cars that 14 kids drove to school. These are not compact cars. They are honest American two-ton machines, all of them aged to perfection before the kids got hold of them. Now, with the last usefulness of this go-round wrung out of them, they're out here waiting for a collector. A huge Buick is missing its hood, and a small tree grows through the engine compartment. The sun glimmers off chrome and hurts the eyes.

An abundance of old farm machinery shows the effects of hard times and hard ground. A vintage threshing machine casts a long shadow.

Al pointed to a spot near the thresher and said, "There's where the rattler got Fred." This was a reference to a story that Al and Fred had told me earlier. Fred, in 1982, after retiring from NASA, was walking along by the thresher and came upon a cat that immediately ran off. It turned out that the cat had been teasing a large rattler, which had gotten so mad it wouldn't even rattle anymore. Then along came Fred and the rattler seized upon his leg as a substitute for the cat.

MICHAEL CRUMMETT

Above: Winter wheat stubble, Big Horn County.
Facing page: Central Montana crop duster.

Nearby cousins took Fred many miles to the hospital and the venom didn't bother him much, but they came close to killing him with the antidote. Such are the memories of life on the farm.

We got back in the diesel Ford and returned to Al's present weathered home. A few woebegone sprigs of corn were standing at odd angles where the hail had left them in Al's garden. "Looks like I'm going to get nothing this year," he said. Normally, he sells vegetables in Poplar, where he finds a ready market. (In my later conversation with Al, he said a few Hubbard squash managed to come back after the hail, but they didn't have time to get very ripe.)

In 1990, Al tried his hand raising kabocha squash for the Japanese. It seemed to have some promise, he said. The Japanese were offering 15 cents a pound. "But then it turned out we had to pay part of the shipping and packaging. This year, they offered us eight cents a pound, which was about the same as we got last year after we paid the packaging and shipping. Then they told us that we still had to pay part of the expenses, so we were only going to actually get six cents a pound. And of course, you have to buy the seeds from them, for about a hundred dollars to the acre. I decided to pass it up. They said I should have been able to grow a semitrailer load, about forty thousand pounds, on four acres. That might have been too much work."

He reflects on the mini-farm that is left to him. "I kept twenty-five acres," he said. "Fourteen acres to grow things, and eleven acres for all my stuff." The rest of his farm and ranch land he had to sell to meet debts. "The place was worth about six hundred thousand dollars and I had borrowed only one hundred thousand dollars, but compounded interest ran my debt to three hundred thousand dollars in ten years. The banks got into trouble because they had overloaned, so they called in payment on loans that didn't have more than fifty percent collateral. that's what low farm prices did to many of us."

Al said losing his place was "the best thing that ever happened to me. I was married to the land. I couldn't imagine being without it. Owning land is an asset and a predicament. The kids didn't mind seeing it go. They said, 'Let it go. It did its job. It raised the family'."

At one point Al was milking cows to help pay his debts, and while he was in the waiting phase of the cow milking, he had time to think. "Usually, working on a farm or ranch, you don't get much time to think. I was in Des Moines to a conference recently, and a lot of the guys there were dairy farmers. They were all telling about ideas they got in their milking parlors. I guess a lot of thinking gets done in milking parlors. Anyway, out there in my milking parlor, I had time to gather some perspective on the benefits of getting free from the land. After I lost my land, I had time to go visit my kids, and to work with farm organizations, all of which I enjoy.

"If I had it to do over, I'd find some way to get away from the land before I had to. And I'd take my kids fishing more. When you get too tied to your work, you neglect your family. I very seldom went fishing with the kids. On one of these places, every time you want to go fishing, you have forty things broke that you have to fix. On my trip to Des Moines, I stopped in Minnesota and visited one of my sons. We have fine conversations now, but I never got to know him until he was grown up. He told me he sure wished I had taken him fishing when he was a boy."

Al said he could have quit farming when he was younger and done any number of other jobs. "I could do anything with machinery, from selling it to fixing it. My dad was a blacksmith, and his dad was a wagon maker back in Wisconsin, so I guess it's a family curse, or blessing, going clear back to Austria."

Al still gets plenty of chances to work with machinery. The people who bought his irrigated land hire him to do a lot of the work. "I do the field work, plant corn, cultivate it, chop it, and haul it to the silage pit. I've got a Bobcat here, and I use it to fix leaks in the irrigation ditch. Sometimes I think maybe the owner should do more of this, but he likes me to do it. It's sort of like hobby farming."

As I was preparing to leave the Schmitz farm, I paused to look over Al's 11 acres of "stuff." It was a wet summer and even the hail hadn't suppressed the lush vegetation. Al's stuff consists of more old machinery, a lot more: a shed, a shop, feedlot, abandoned milking parlor, and an old trailer house that is used to accommodate overflow visitors.

Just beyond Al's stuff and some trees, the Missouri runs as slow and placid as time itself. The glassy surface reflects the green bank on the other side and the white trunks of the cottonwoods. Several wild geese skim upriver just above the surface, their reflections keeping time.

On the porch of his house, Al is optimistic. "People have been leaving here for a long time, but now they're coming back. Maybe the kids will come back."

JOHN REDDY

"People have been leaving here for a long time, but now they're coming back."

MICHAEL CRUMMETT

Helen Waller does not mince words when she talks about family farms. "The family farm is basic to the democratic system," she said. "It is not only a good way of life but the foundation for a wide dispersal of land ownerships."

The definition of a family farm, she said, is a farm where family members make the decisions. Her interest in family farming is more than academic. She and her husband Gordon operate a wheat and barley farm near Circle. Their modest farm buildings look out over rolling fields of green and gold. On the pleasant July day when I visited the Waller farm, two large, dual-wheeled John Deere tractors were sitting in front of the steel Quonset machine shop, facing the fields as though they might roar out at any moment. There was the space and silence that you find only when you are far from town. The only movement was a gentle prairie breeze that was making just the faintest rustling in some dried grass.

"I have my own forty-three–foot tool bar," Helen told me proudly. A "tool bar," as I was informed, is an implement that can be outfitted with a variety of different tools for working the soil. The most common tool is the "duckfoot," the basic cultivation tool of dryland grain farming. Each duckfoot shovel is V-shaped, and somebody imagined it looked like the foot of a duck, pointed backwards. The duckfoot is used to loosen the soil before planting, and to get rid of weeds during the summer. Pulling a duckfoot on fallow land to get rid of weeds is referred to as "summer fallowing."

"My husband and I have worked together pretty successfully as a team. I do the things he doesn't like to do, and he does what I can't do. I like to summer fallow, for example, and I do all the book work. He does the maintenance on the machinery. He drives the combine, I haul the grain to the bins. I do farm work because I like it. This doesn't mean my job is 'driving tractor.' Farming is a way of life, rather than a job."

Helen is active in the National Family Farm Coalition, which operates in 35 states. The coalition provides "long-term advocacy of an adequate food supply," she said. Her work with this organization, along with her experience on her own family's farm, has given her insight into the big problems facing family-scale agriculture.

"All over this country there are farms that have been forced out of business. They went out of business because their costs kept going up while their income went down. In 1973, it took fifteen calves to buy a pickup. Last year, it took forty calves. In 1975, it took four thousand bushel of wheat to buy a tractor. Now it costs twelve thousand bushel. Farmers have no control of prices. Their only choice is whether to join the farm program. The program is voluntary, if you don't mind going broke the next year."

The program also places various controls on farmers. "Take wetlands protection for example. If you're in the program, you can't drain your bog holes." Other farm programs also have problems. For example, Helen said, the Conservation Reserve Program, which pays farmers to take marginal land out of production for 10 years, is enormously expensive for the taxpayer. "Some people are getting more than they paid for the land," she said. Payments in Montana range from $32 per acre per year to $45. "There are lots of cheaper ways the same thing could have been accomplished."

She pointed out that the grain trade is in the hands of a monopoly, with only five companies handling all the grain worldwide. "The same situation is building in the meat packing business. A few large companies run the food supply. Last year, food processors paid investors a forty-two percent return."

Financial reports in December 1991 indicated that food processing and manufacturing companies were among the most lucrative investments in the U.S. that year. "Contrast that to the farmer who is getting paid less than it costs to grow raw materials. Nothing is going to change until urban

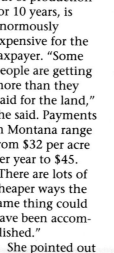

Helen Waller—Circle
Limit Production Rather than Acreage

and rural people alike realize food is a basic commodity. The awakening will come when grocery stores start to have less food available."

Helen said it is not surprising that nonfarm people are not concerned about the condition of farmers. "Urban people have just as many problems. The wolf is at their door, too."

Government efforts to help farmers fall short, Helen said. "The farm subsidy program does not benefit the producers. It theoretically benefits food buyers, and the taxpayers pick up the difference. So people pay less for their food but pay more taxes." Further, she said, the farm program does not encourage food quality, or benefit the environment. Under the program, farmers are limited to the number of acres they can farm. This causes farmers to use more chemicals than they might like to use in order to maximize production on that set acreage.

"If Congress were to limit each farmer's production rather than acreage, it would be the best environmental bill they could pass. We could farm less intensively on more acres. People are getting concerned about food quality. Soil conservation measures also should be factored into the farm program, so that farmers are encouraged to conserve their soil."

Big-time corporate farming, which is sometimes suggested as a replacement for smaller family farms, certainly is no friend of the environment, Helen said. Workers on a big corporate farm are not likely to be concerned about long-term problems that their operations might cause, such as erosion. That's one reason why family farms are always going to be competitive, she said.

Besides concerns about the quality of food, Helen pointed out that the family farming way of life has positive values in itself. "We brought up five kids here," she said. "Kids growing up on a farm learn the value of work. They learn that they have to produce, deliver the goods." For a lot of people, the alternative to working on a farm is working for the government. "Those are mainly a lot of leech jobs," she said. The Waller children have all grown and left home, except for one son who is working to take over part of the farm.

Because of present farm conditions, "We are losing a whole generation of farmers. These are the most efficient and best educated farmers, between twenty-five and thirty-five years old. A lot of them would like to stay, but they can't."

Politics is not the answer to farm problems, Helen said. "Farmers in trouble run the political spectrum from liberal-liberal to conservative-conservative. They're all in the same boat. Politicians are political animals. The big agribusiness PACs buy their votes. Congress is too far gone. The process is just so violated. There is a whale of a wreck coming, and I think, in my case, that there is a lot of virtue in just sitting back and waiting for it to happen. When it does happen, I'm going to be glad to be living on a farm.

"Farmers cannot permanently continue to sell their crops for less than it costs to raise them. Right now, a lot of farmers are limping along with equipment that ought to be retired, just because they can't afford to buy new equipment. When these implements are finally beyond repair, and when enough land has gone out of production into CRP, and the population has increased enough and is demanding more food, then something will happen."

Meantime, Helen says, life on the farm continues to provide many satisfactions. Happiness comes from liking your work, she said. "There is a lot of satisfaction in watching nature. Farmers like to watch things grow. They are happy working the land, producing a product essential to civilization. And as for me, I like the peace and quiet."

Haying along the Musselshell River near Harlowton.

TOM DIETRICH

My initial interview with Dena Hoff was not restful. It was in July, and July is not a restful time around the Hoff farm six miles southwest of Glendive. There is no restful time around the Hoff farm. When I found Mrs. Hoff, she and various women and children from her extended family were hoeing a beanfield. The famous eastern Montana sun was pounding down on the beanfield and the people looked tiny and half lost in the shimmer under the hot sky. On two sides of the beanfield, deep green field corn was soaking up the sun, well on its way to being as tall as an elephant's eye. At the end of the field were a couple of well-used vehicles. One was an American car of the oxidized two-ton vintage, where a kid was keeping an eye on a baby. Neither of them was very happy.

When I caught up to Dena in mid-field, she didn't stop but said she didn't mind talking, as long as I didn't get in the way or slow down her hoeing. So I hopped along the adjoining row asking questions about farming, pausing to yank up the occasional big weed growing in my row.

Dena's view of farming is not a happy one. "The family farm is an endangered species. The public doesn't value us at all. They are perfectly willing to let us work ourselves to death so they can have cheap food. People need to realize that all food has somebody's blood, sweat and tears on it."

Later, Dena told me of a Christmas party she attended in Texas, where most of those attending were college professors and other professional level workers. "They told me how glad they were to meet a farmer, how they'd never met a farmer before. They said how wonderful it must be to be out there with nature and animals. I told them about the problems of farmers, and they had never heard of any of them. I told them I had wanted to meet some Texas farmers, but wasn't able to, because of scheduling problems. They said, 'Why would you want to meet any of those people. I don't think you'd want to talk to any of them.'

"Farming has two problems. Poor image, and bad prices. People who aren't farmers see us as someone they have to subsidize with tax money. People in the city are so removed. They think food comes from stores. As far as the bad prices, that's caused by the entire food processing business being in very few hands. The chicken growers are some of the most monopolized, and some of them have said they are serfs on their own land."

Dena Hoff and her husband Alvin work harder than people ought to, but they are not serfs yet. At their farm, located on the bank of the Yellowstone, they raise sheep, corn, dry beans, alfalfa, and grain, mostly barley. All their crop land is irrigated.

The Hoffs bought their farm 11 years ago after coming over from western North Dakota. Both the Hoffs are from nonagricultural backgrounds, but "We always wanted to be farmers," Dena said. Alvin Hoff works as a conductor on the railroad, but his shifts vary unpredictably, making it difficult for him to work on the farm the way he would like to. "Sometimes when he goes he's gone for twenty-four hours or it might only be eight hours. You never know," Dena said. Nevertheless, the Hoffs and a few helpful relatives do all the work on their farm except for combining their grain and corn, which they hire someone to do.

The week after Christmas, I telephoned Dena to find out how her year had gone, and asked her to tell me some of the yearly round of activities on her farm.

"Well, right now we are cleaning up our paperwork, paying year-end bills, planning and budgeting for the next year. We have to plan how many acres of what we are going to grow, and how much of what sorts of inputs, fertilizer and such, we are going to need. We have to make alternative plans, plan A, plan B, plan C, for when we go into the bank to get financing for next year's operation.

"And of course there is the normal routine work that goes on every day all year; feeding the sheep, milking the cows and taking care of the poultry. In an open winter like this one is so far, we can also work on our fences and corrals. There's always a lot of odd jobs. For example, today we killed hogs and my husband and a friend of his are cleaning out the entrails to make sausage casings. Also, we've been wildly plucking ducks, geese and chickens. We sell all these locally. There are always plenty of people standing in line to buy them. We also had fifty turkeys this year.

DANIEL N. VICHOREK

Dena Hoff—Glendive
FAMILY FARM IS AN ENDANGERED SPECIES

"This year we expect to start lambing in late February. We're lambing in February because during the excitement of my son's birthday party earlier this year, a gate got left open and the rams got in with the ewes a little early. Normally we start lambing in the second week of March. Lambing for us entails staying up all night and living in the barn. This goes on for about three weeks.

"Then, we start getting ready for planting. We buy our

JUDITH STROM

seed, and if it is an open spring, we might be able to start some fieldwork. Plowing, leveling, discing. Exactly what we do and when we do it depends on the weather and what we are going to plant. We were late planting last year because of the rain. The rain also meant we didn't have to worry about irrigating as soon as we would have to in a dry year. In real dry years, we turn the water in the field in April and don't quit irrigating until the end of September. Those years, it seems you just get to water to the end of the field and its time to go back and start again.

"If it's a year when we're going to plant alfalfa, we'll get it planted as soon as we can work the ground, maybe in March, weather permitting. Once the alfalfa is in, you start preparing the field for the row crops. Land that is going into row crops has to be worked over and over again, plowed, disced, and leveled." ("Leveling" consists of grading the surface to a gentle slope away from the source of the irrigation water.)

"Generally you have to level whenever you plow. We try to plant the grain in April or May, as soon as we can, considering the weather. Corn and beans go in a little later, but should be in by the middle of May. And of course while you're doing all this you have to be planting your garden and hoeing the shelterbelt around the buildings and replacing any plants that have died in the shelterbelt. These gardening and shelterbelt chores usually take about a week. Then sometime in the spring, depending on the weather, you have to get ready to irrigate. You have to get out your canvas dams and your gated pipe and your siphons and whatever else you need. You have to plow ditches if they are needed. Even before this it might be time to irrigate the sheep pasture.

"In May, the baby chickens, geese, ducks and turkeys arrive and have to be taken care of. Somewhere in this time frame, depending on the weather, it is time to cultivate the row crops. Usually we pull a ditcher behind the cultivator. The ditcher makes a trench between rows to carry irrigation water.

"Before the end of June, it should be time for the first cutting of hay. This takes about two weeks. At the same time there are potatoes and shelterbelt trees that have to be hoed, and animals that have to be wormed, inoculated, and moved around.

"In July the grain is harvested. Also in July, and early August, we hoe the beans. In late August, if the weather lets us, we cut the beans into windrows to let them dry until they can be combined. About this time we also have to water the pasture, and in among everything else will be the second and third cuttings of hay. We combine the beans whenever they get dry enough.

"In September we put the lambs in a separate pasture and start feeding them corn to put on weight before we sell them. At the same time, we condition our ewes for breeding by feeding them corn for at least seventeen days before breeding begins. This feeding results in what we call 'flushing.' This means that ovulation is increased. Our goal is to increase multiple births.

"In late September or early October the corn should get dry enough to cut. You can either wait for it to dry to fifteen percent moisture in the field and then combine it, or you can cut it at moisture up to twenty-three percent and use dryers on it. The dryers are fueled with propane and almost nobody uses them anymore. Sometimes bad weather doesn't let the corn dry enough to combine, or you don't get to it, or it gets snowed in, and then people will be combining in the spring. You lose a lot of corn when you have to combine in the spring. Deer and raccoons do a lot of damage over the winter."

Also in the fall are the numerous miscellaneous maintenance chores; "cleaning barns and corrals, spreading manure on the fields if you don't have several feet of snow, winterizing equipment, putting things away. And then we sell the lambs. After that, it's into the year-end phase again."

Dena told me that all these events vary wildly in their timing because of weather and unexpected events. "We never have an average anything around here," she said. "We get up in the morning with an idea of what we are going to do, but we may or may not get it done. We are never exactly on a schedule."

I told Dena that her annual routine sounded exhausting to me. I asked her where she took her satisfaction from it. "Well, we like to work," she said. "It is pretty discouraging, though, to work hard to get a good crop and then not get paid for it."

I mentioned that another sheep grower had told me that her operation improved its situation by breeding finer wool to get a better price, and Dena said they had done that too, but not to much avail. "The trouble is that Australia and New Zealand have a monster surplus that could supply all the wool for the world, without even looking at the U.S crop, which isn't that much."

I asked Dena if she and her husband ever considered hiring migrant workers to hoe their beans. She said they come to work the sugar beets early in the year, and are usually gone by the time the beans need work. "Besides that, they cost too much." Nonmigrant workers are not much help either. "Sometimes we get somebody out here, and by mid-afternoon they look at their watch and say, 'Oh my, is it two already? I have to go to my dentist appointment.' And we don't see them again." So she and her family members do all the work themselves, with help from a faithful brother-in-law and a cousin of her husband.

I told her that hoeing those beans was the hardest work I saw on my travels for this book. "You weren't there long enough," she said. "We could have given you a hoe."

"I was afraid of sunstroke," I said.

"That's why we wear floppy hats and long-sleeve shirts and drink lots of water."

I asked Dena if the Hoff farm was going to come out all right in the end. "I'm sort of guarded about that right now," she said. "We're trying to restructure our financing...we'll just have to see. All we've ever wanted is to pay for this place and keep ourselves fed and pay our taxes. We'd like to get up to the subsistence level. I often think how nice it would be if we could just work and not have to deal with bankers and all the manipulation."

The two of Dena's children remaining at home are not enthusiastic about farming, she said. "They see kids in town laying around, doing nothing, or whatever they want to do, and they compare this to ten hours in the bean field and it doesn't look too good."

At the end of our conversation in December I asked Dena how she had come out with the beans from that overheated field where I first interviewed her. "Oh, we lost all of them. Yes. It rained on the windrows in September and October and ruined them. They were worth about twelve thousand dollars." ■

MICHAEL CRUMMETT

Above: Lamb twins.
Facing page: Sheep and their guard donkey, Broadwater County.

"Lambing for us entails staying up all night and living in the barn. This goes on for about three weeks."

*Below: Jim Courtney
Facing page: Near
Horton.*

DANIEL N. VICHOREK

Jim Courtney—Alzada
Government Controls Are the Worst Problem

A world of grass." That's a rancher's dream, and it's the highest praise they can give to ranching conditions. Traveling around Montana in the summer of 1991, I was reminded that a little rainfall turns much of the state's rangeland into a world of grass. Nowhere was this more true in my travels that year than on Jim Courtney's ranch near Alzada.

"This is good grass too," Jim told me. "It's mostly western wheat grass and green needle grass. Cattle get fat on it, and it keeps its quality all winter. Nine years out of ten, we graze the cattle all winter. The tenth year, we get snowed in."

Normally, the Alzada country only gets 11 or 12 inches of rain, Jim said. Nevertheless, the moisture is ample to grow a good stand of dryland hay, a mix of crested wheat and alfalfa. The Courtney ranch buildings look out over a rolling country that was mostly green when I visited in July. Large round hay bales were distributed in long lines that ran off toward the horizon in various directions. There were no fences to mar the view. It looked to me as though they could cut hay about anywhere, probably clear into Wyoming or South Dakota, which are not far away. It looked like a ranching paradise to me.

"There's a lot of downs in the ranching business," Jim said. "There's drought and grasshoppers and the rest, but we don't get much of that here." Still, Jim said that 1991 didn't have enough precipitation to fill the stock-watering reservoirs. "I look for a lot of wells and pipelines in this country," he said. "It's a long-term solution for droughty conditions."

With no immediate worries of being 'hoppered or dried out, Jim is free to worry about problems from far away. "Government controls are the worst problem. People who write the laws have no feel for what it is like out here on the land. Max Baucus has proposed changes to the Clean Water Act that would totally upset ranching operations. But the worst law they've ever passed is the Endangered Species Act. If I shoot a wolf that's harassing my horses, I'm eligible for a fine of a hundred thousand dollars and a year in jail. They're trying to reintroduce the black-footed ferret in Blaine County. If they do, forty or fifty ranching operations are going to be threatened.

"Agriculture is the biggest business in Montana and in the country, but we're losing people and losing representation. In the Montana Legislature, only forty percent of the members have any ties to agriculture. Another thing is, we're getting more and more pressure from animal rights groups to not do things we have to do. They don't want us to castrate or brand our calves, for example.

"Our biggest challenge is to convince the American public that we do a good job with range management and the land resources. Right now, people have doubts. We have to get out there and sell our image."

A major element of the campaign to sell the ranchers' image is the Beef Check-off Fund, which receives one dollar from every head of cattle sold in the U.S. This fund takes in as much as $90 million a year, and is earmarked for beef promotion and research. "A lot of research has been done on the nutrition value of beef, for example. As a result of this, we now have the American Medical Association telling people that lean beef is good for them. As part of this effort to make beef more popular, I and many others in the beef industry have worked to breed 'growthier,' leaner cattle that produce the cuts that today's consumer wants. Ranchers need to be aware of the best sort of cattle for today's market conditions.

"The grass-roots people need to come alive if we are going to continue in business. We need to work a little harder to elect a legislature that understands our problems. We need tax incentives. The growers have things they need to do too. They need to limit the number of cattle available in order to help keep the price up. We need to be sure we are selling the product the public wants, and we have to maintain a good inspection system to make sure quality is maintained. And we need to do something about our education system. In Billings, for example, the biggest city in the state, there is not a single class on agriculture in the public schools."

Regarding the changes that confront agriculture in the state, Jim said there is a trend to absentee landowners that sometimes benefits the local community and sometimes hurts it. He cited the case of Drew Lewis, a member of the Reagan cabinet, who came to southeast Montana to go hunting, saw a "ranch for sale" sign, and bought it on the spot. Then he built a big house there and he comes and spends a week or two a year.

There is another trend; Jim called it a "scary trend" for groups such as the Nature Conservancy and the Department of Fish Wildlife and Parks to buy up ranches and turn them over to the Bureau of Land Management to be managed for recreational purposes. "We are losing our tax base. There are too many projects where the government winds up owning land."

Despite all these problems, Jim said he is optimistic about the future of ranching. "I think we'll be okay if we can hold off some of the worse legislation." Jim has been a rancher all his life, and his family has lived on this same ranch since his father originally leased it in 1929. He and his wife raised five children there, and one son probably will take over the place eventually, he said. "Ranching gets to be a part of you....I don't know what I would be doing if I wasn't ranching. I don't know anything else."

Jim said the members of his family don't feel that they necessarily miss anything just because they are 500 miles from Helena. "Well, I suppose we do miss a few things. These small towns don't provide the services. Ekalaka doesn't have an implement dealer anymore. Baker used to have several, and now it has one. CRP [Conservation Reservation Program] has hurt implement dealers all over the state. Having to go farther to get to an implement dealer raises the ranchers' costs."

Jim is not impressed by the trend of ranchers growing exotic cattle. "We tried 'em," he said. "We had calving problems, and they used too much feed." The Courtney ranch grows purebred registered Hereford bulls. "It's not much different than a cow-calf operation," he said. "We have to keep a little better records, we have to know what bull bred what cow, for example, to keep the bloodlines straight." The Courtneys recently had a bull sale, Jim said, and their bulls brought up to $6,000 apiece.

Jim said the high-quality lifestyle of Montana will continue to bring in more people to some regions. "People look at Montana as the last place to go. It's a very diverse state. We would like to preserve the lifestyle, the quiet, free life. We don't mind paying our rightful share of the taxes to stay where we are." ▪

TOM DIETRICH

WAYNE MUMFORD

Ed Lord and his wife Connie raise premium beef cattle in the high altitude of the Flint Creek Valley south of Philipsburg. Their ranch is on the postcard-pretty rise of land that leads the eye up to the Pintler Range. "This is late-spring country," Ed said, referring to the long winter that comes with the 5,700-foot altitude.

Ed said he has seen a lot of changes since he leased the ranch from his father in 1960. Perhaps the most basic example has been the evolution of haying equipment. In 1960, when Ed took over, all the hay was put up with beaverslide stackers. Beaverslides are those home-made high-rise wooden devices made mostly of poles that are still used in the Big Hole, Nevada Creek valley near Ovando, and a few other places where boggy fields or other conditions warrant their use. Operation of a beaverslide and the other equipment that goes with it, dump rakes, buckrakes and so on, requires a crew of several men. As time has gone on, equipment has become more expensive to purchase but has eliminated most of the labor connected with haying.

On the Lord ranch, the first major step away from the beaverslide technology was the hay baler that made small rectangular bales. These bales were never picked by hand here. Instead, Ed built a steel sled to pull behind the baler. A hired hand rode this sled and piled the bales into a 13-bale configuration that matched the pickup head on Ed's hydraulic loader. When the 13 bales were accumulated, the hired hand stuck a steel bar into the ground through a slot that ran the length of the sled. As the sled kept moving, the bar slid the bales off the back. "This was hard work," Ed said. "We needed a good hand. The bales kept coming as he was sliding the pile off, and if the hay was heavy and dry the bales really kept coming." After the baling was done, Ed went around the field with his loader and picked up the 13-bale piles and placed them on a wagon, which hauled them to a feeding area near the buildings.

It was important to move the hay to the feeding area before winter, because bad weather could block the hay-hauling road as fast as it could be plowed and make it nearly impossible to get the cattle fed. City people who are accustomed to "calling in sick" in bad weather, or even if they are sick, may have difficulty understanding that there is no such option as "not feeding the cattle." No matter who is sick or how bad the weather is, cattle must be fed every day in winter.

After using this system for a while, Ed switched back to the beaverslide, because making small bales was slow and expensive. It became easier to move the loose hay stacked with the beaverslide after Ed built a stack mover that could move a whole loose hay stack weighing between 12 and 15 tons. The stack mover design was based on a smaller unit that Ed had seen a picture of, though the scale-up presented some problems. "I wrecked the first four or five I built," Ed said. The one that finally worked used a three-quarter-inch cable and a winch with a 200-to-1 ratio to pull the stack onto the mover, which was mounted on two truck axles.

The stack mover was successful, but had a lot of critical parts that could break if they were not operated just so. For this reason, Ed felt that he had to be personally on hand when the stack mover was used. As Ed got more involved with matters off the ranch and had to be away more, an easier way was needed to move the stacks. The answer was a new machine called a Haybuster. This machine took hay out of the windrow and moved it by conveyor into a round cage that was pulled behind the tractor. This made a compact three- to four-ton stack that could be moved with a commercial stack mover.

The haybuster worked well, but also had a lot of moving parts that caused more down time than could be tolerated. Ed went back to his shop and built a three-sided cage that could be used as a form to make 16x24-foot rectangular stacks that could be moved with the commercial stack mover. The cage required almost as much crew as a beaverslide because buckrakes were needed to bring the hay in to the Farmhand hydraulic loader that lifted the hay into the cage.

The Lord ranch used this low-tech method for a few years, and then one of the neighbors got a baler that made big round bales. At first there was no easy way to feed cattle with these bales, but then a machine was developed to turn the bale and slice a six-inch thick peel of hay off and spew it out the side where cattle could get it. Ed still uses the commercial stack mover, which moves 12 of the round 1,100-pound bales at once. The haying crew, which once had up to five men, has diminished to a single person who, if necessary, can handle all the

Ed and Connie Lord—
Flint Creek Valley
The Right Cattle and the Right Processes

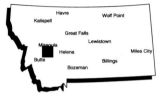

operations one by one. Rather than one person doing all the work, though, Ed and his hired man and one temporary employee usually put up the thousand tons of hay that the Lord ranch grows each year.

The Lords' present system is not necessarily the last word in hay technology. "I'm always looking for an easier way," Ed said. "By easier, I mean that it takes either less time or labor, or both."

BOB & MARLYS SELL

Above: On the Red Rocks Game Refuge.
Facing page: Range below the Pintler Range.

During my visit to the Lord ranch, Ed and Connie took me out to look at some of their fine, sleek and shiny cattle. "These days," Ed said, we don't talk about 'fat cattle,' or 'slaughter cattle.' We talk about 'finished cattle,' or 'feeder cattle'."

Ed and Connie's cows are all at least half Black Angus. Their bulls are Charolais, a French breed with white hair and dark skin. This produces a bunch of calves with colors varying from pure white to dark gray. I asked Ed and Connie how they knew this was the right kind of cattle.

"You can't be sentimental about cattle," Ed said, referring to the attachment some cattlemen have for some traditional breeds that are not suited for modern ranch and market conditions. "Climatic conditions are one limitation on cattle. The 'right cattle' in Texas probably are not going to be the 'right cattle' in Montana. 'Right cattle' are going to be different in different parts of the country." Ed told me that his cattle are about right for his particular situation.

The Angus cows are good for a variety of reasons, he said. For one thing, Angus cows have good "maternal qualities." They take good care of their calves, have a good udder shape and produce ample milk. The black skin on the udder of an Angus will not sunburn, even when the sun reflects brightly off the snow. This is important because a cow with a sunburned udder will not allow her calf to nurse, which causes problems. Ed raised Hereford cattle before he began raising Angus, and he remembered that they are famous among cattlemen for their sunburned udders. "These cattle I've got now are adaptable to the climate," Ed said. The Charolais crossbreed produces an offspring that readily fattens to "choice" grade in the feedlot, he added.

As owner/operators of a family cow-calf ranch operation and veteran cattle growers, Ed and Connie are optimistic about the future of their business. "The export potential for beef is great," Ed said. He said increasing world-wide affluence will cause people in foreign countries to want beef, and to have the money to buy it. Other good news for the western cattle rancher, Ed explained, is that cattle-growing in other areas of the country, particularly the Midwest, is passing from the scene. "There's a new generation of young farmers in the Midwest that aren't interested in cattle," Ed said, "maybe because they are too much hassle." These days, he said, midwestern farmers mostly just plow their leftover cornstalks back into the ground, rather than feeding them to cattle as they once did. These non-livestock farmers are referred to as "CB&F," farmers, standing for "corn, beans, and Florida." Florida evidently is where most young farmers would rather be than feeding cattle in a blizzard.

Despite the loss of much of the midwestern cow/calf industry, cattle raising in the U.S. is still mostly a small-scale undertaking much different from the bigger western operations, Ed said. "The average cow herd in the U.S. is thirty-six head. Less than five percent of the people who raise cattle make their whole living doing it."

Ed thinks the future of western-style cattle raising is going to depend on an increasing degree of "vertical integration," wherein the stockgrower is involved in more than just growing the calf to a certain size and then selling it to a feeder.

"Chickens and pigs are our competition, and we're never going to be as vertically integrated as they are. A contract chicken grower takes a company-owned bird from a baby chick to the market-ready stage in forty-nine days. The company then kills it, dresses it, packs it, and sends it to the supermarket ready to be sold. All the supermarket does is open the box and put it out for sale.

"In the beef business, the rancher usually sells his calves to a feeder, who feeds them grain in a feedlot until they get to where they will grade 'choice.' Then the feeder sells them to a packer, who slaughters them, cuts them into large pieces, and sends them to the retail stores.

"I think this is going to change. When ranchers develop genetically superior cattle that will reach the 'choice' grade more economically than other cattle, it is going to benefit the rancher to retain ownership of those cattle when he sends them to the feeder. Then, when they're ready to slaughter, the feeder sells them for you. The rancher benefits because the superior genetics require less time and feed to get them up to 'choice' than it would take other cattle. Less time on feed means less cost means more profit for the owner when they sell. Cattle are not slaughtered until they grade 'choice.' 'Choice' refers to the amount and pattern of fat marbling the meat.

"It's in regard to the raising of cattle that vegetarians get off the track," Ed explained. "They claim that raising cattle for beef is wasteful because cattle eat grain that people could eat. What they never seem to realize is that for most of a beef animal's life it lives on grass, which is not edible for humans. Cattle convert inedible grass to meat.

"At present, packers ship beef to retailers in boxes. This is called 'box beef.' One box may contain whole chucks that will be cut into chuck roasts and steaks, another might contain whole loins that will be cut into T-bones, and so on. Each store has its own meat cutter who trims the fat to the standard set by the store, and cuts the pieces the way the store or a particular customer wants them. The customer never knows where any of this meat comes from. You go back behind the counter and you see boxes of beef from four or five different packers.

"I think before long we're going to see 'branded beef.' This will be beef with a brand name on it to ensure the consumer of uniform taste and size of cuts. This 'branded' beef will be cut up before it is sent to the retail stores, and will be ready to sell when it gets there, just like chicken. One thing this means is that you're not going to have a meat cutter any more at your Safeway store in Anaconda, Montana, for example.

"Right now, the biggest complaint about beef is that the cuts tend to be non-uniform in size and taste. Consumers want a given cut of beef to be the same size and have the same taste time after time. Uniformity is difficult to achieve because of the variation in cattle. The ideal weight of a dressed beef carcass, the size that produces the size of cuts the housewife wants, is seven hundred to seven hundred fifty pounds. A carcass this size normally requires a live weight of about eleven hundred to twelve hundred pounds. However, some cattle won't grade 'choice' when they reach twelve hundred pounds, so they have to be fed longer. Say

a steer doesn't reach 'choice' until it weighs fourteen hundred and fifty pounds. A carcass that size is going to have T-bones and other cuts that will be much larger than most housewives want. With selective breeding, we can produce cattle that when fed properly will usually grade 'choice' at about twelve hundred pounds. That will enhance the uniformity that consumers want and make the product more attractive."

Ed readily admits that a rancher retaining ownership of his cattle while they are at the finishing stage is a low level of "vertical integration" as compared to the chicken and pork business. Even that low level will stick in the craw of some cattlemen, he said. "I'm not saying I like it. A lot of my neighbors don't like it either. I just think a certain amount of it is inevitable. We have to take our cue from the more efficient industries."

WAYNE MUMFORD

Not to be left behind, Ed and Connie currently retain ownership of some of their calves through the finishing stage.

"The nature of the cattle business is always going to be different from the pig or chicken business," Ed said, adding "we're never going to compete with a forty-nine-day chicken." Still, he said, cattle that sell for 70 cents a pound will produce hamburger that is cheaper than chicken, if you only consider the edible portion of the whole chicken. "Basically, we have a Cadillac product that people are willing to pay a premium price for. We're eating all we raise at a reasonable price. Most other segments of agriculture have the government involved to the point where supply and demand don't dictate prices. And this is a product that can be improved. That's part of the reason I am optimistic."

Ed pointed out that at one time in the past there were

Good news for the western cattle rancher is that cattle-growing in other areas of the country, particularly the Midwest, is passing from the scene.

130 million beef cattle in the U.S., and although that number is now down to 100 million, the amount of beef produced is still the same. This is because of genetic improvements and better management, he said.

Ed and Connie said that family-size cattle ranches are probably the best way to grow beef cattle in the Flint Creek valley. "These are intensive management operations with lots of irrigation," Ed said. "Big ranches that have to hire help have a hard time getting it. Nobody wants to work these long hours unless they own the place."

The Lords said that the ownership of cattle ranches in the upper Flint Creek drainage has been stable over the years. "A lot of these families have been here for three generations," Connie said.

The Lords noted there are only two absentee landowners in the upper Flint Creek valley. One big ranch in the vicinity "never really worked as a big ranch," Ed said, but the ranch was then split up and sold to five different local ranchers who have been quite successful incorporating the pieces into their operations. The Lord ranch was one of the buyers.

On my September visit, Ed took me out to look at one of the interesting aspects of his operation, which is a series of gravity-fed center pivot sprinklers. Because of the slope of the Lords' land, they can pipe water from their ditch to these sprinklers, which apply it to the land without any need for pumps. "You need fifty vertical feet of head to operate the sprinklers," Ed said. Electric motors move these systems around their pivots at a rate that can be set by the operator. Ed sets his systems to apply two inches of water every eight days. The minimum time for a complete rotation is 19½ hours. "This is an example of improved management," Ed said. He said the land under the sprinkler produces three tons of hay to the acre, compared to two tons for the flood irrigation that he previously used on the same land.

I asked Ed my customary question about what it takes to be a success in farming or ranching today. "First off," he said, "you need to be a mechanic. After that, you need good people-management skills, you need to be a good business-man, you need some education beyond high school, and you need awareness of the industry you are in. To get some of this awareness, you need to travel and talk to people. And most of all, you need to like what you're doing. One thing to remember: if you want to succeed, watch somebody who is successful, and see how he did it."

Ed is in a good position to fulfill the traveling and talking requirements, because he travels widely in connection with his duties as a vice president of the Montana Stockgrowers Association and as a member of the National Beef Promotion and Research Board. This board oversees the use of the money raised for beef promotion by the Beef Check-off Fund.

Another route to awareness of the cattle business is Cattlefax, a data service which is a subsidiary of the National Cattlemen's Association. Subscribers to this service get a weekly printout showing what cattle have sold for during the previous week, and they get access to an 800 number that will put them in touch with an analyst for up-to-the-minute information. When subscribers sell cattle, they inform the fax service of the price and other details.

Ed said ranchers need to stay politically active. "Every rancher should be a member of the Montana Stockgrowers and National Cattlemen's Association."

Given the Lords' enthusiasm for their business, I asked them who was going to take over their ranch when they are gone. They have two grown children who are out in the world, and neither of them has shown any interest in taking over the ranch. "Well, they could change their minds," Ed said.

Below: In the Tobacco Root Mountains.
Facing page: Near Lolo.

TOM DIETRICH

JOHN REDDY

Charles Swanson lives in the house that his grandfather built when he came to the Bitter-root to homestead in 1909. Charles' grandfather was named Charles too, so there is a nice sense of continuity.

Besides building a house, the original Charles Swanson planted 10 acres of Macintosh apples, which continue to produce unto the present day. The son of the first Charles Swanson, who also is the father of the present Charles

DANIEL N. VICHOREK

Charles and Julie Swanson
IDEAL CONDITIONS FOR APPLES

Swanson, operated the original orchard and expanded into the commercial beef cow business. The present Charles Swanson came out of military service in 1970 and saw that the family farm needed some new ideas. On the apple side of the business, he decided to plant two new orchards. This he did, planting one in 1975 and another in 1978, which, along with the original orchard, brought the total up to 25 acres. Today, the Swanson orchards produce 8,000 to 10,000 bushels of apples per year. About 80 percent of these are Macintosh. The remainder are Viking, Paulen Red, Wealthy, Red Delicious, Golden Delicious, and Spartan. All the non-Macintosh serve as pollinators for the Macs. Every fifth row of trees is pollina-tors.

The pollinator apples are sold through grocery stores within 100 miles. The Macs are sold up to 250 miles away, mostly through stores in Missoula, Butte, Bozeman, Great Falls, and Helena. Charles delivers the apples himself, pulling a gooseneck trailer behind a diesel-powered pickup. The price of the Macs depends primarily on their size. The Swansons retail their "orchard run" apples for 25 cents a pound, which comes to $10 for a 40-pound bushel.

The Swansons also press 6,000 to 8,000 gallons of cider from Macintosh apples. While it lasts, this cider sells at the rate of about 500 gallons per week in Missoula stores, and some is sold through stores farther west. Most of the cider

the Swansons make is produced from apples grown in the old orchard planted by Charles' grandfather back in 1909. Pound for pound, Charles said, the apples from the old orchard contain far more juice than those from the new.

The less juicy nature of the newer apples is partly a result of horticultural selection, Charles said. He said that horti-culturists developing new strains of apples tend to concen-trate on improving size, appearance, and the shipability of apples. Concentrating on these qualities can lead to the loss of others, such as juiciness. Charles suggested that the development of the Red Delicious apple was a sort of culmination of the horticulturists' art. "It looks great, ships great, and tastes terrible," he said.

These days, Charles said, horticulturists expect an orchard to have 15 to 20 years of top productivity. After that, the size of apples is expected to decline. "It's just like you," Charles said. "When you were seventeen or eighteen, you had more endurance and stamina by far than you had when you were forty. Good-quality large apples are going to come from a younger tree. Most of our customers want smaller apples. About two and three-quarters inches is usually what they want. But we have fewer larger apples. A few years ago we used to have enough larger apples to sell what we call 'gift box apples' that people could give for Christmas presents. We don't have that size apples any-more."

Another factor operating in determining the size of apples is the weather, which makes the Swanson apples generally smaller than the same varieties grown elsewhere. For example, Red Delicious, surely one of the most familiar types of apples here, grows only to about half the normal supermarket size. Without the coating of wax that normally comes with them, the Red Delicious in the Swansons' orchard, with their fine sheen of natural apple dust, are hardly recognizable. I proved to myself that they also are much more tasty than the usual store-bought variety.

All in all, Charles told me, the payback on apples is a little better than on cattle. He said about 40 percent of the family income derives from the 25 acres of apples on the 500 acres of land they own. To improve the payback on the cattle, the Swansons have sunk a good deal of cash into upgrading their stock.

"We have about a hundred and seventy cows now, black baldy crosses [Black Angus crossed with Herefords to produce a black animal with a white face] crossed with Limousin bulls. This produces calves that grow fast. We have our own feedlots. We pull the calves off their mothers in November, hold them six or eight weeks until they weigh eight hundred pounds."

One thing the cattle eat in the feedlot is the apple pulp left over after cider is pressed out. "They almost knock over the fence to get it," one of the Swanson's workers told me.

Charles Swanson told me that growing apples is a labor-intensive operation. Winter pruning goes on from-mid February until April. Summer pruning and thinning begin in May, and require about one week each month. Spraying and fertilizing begin in May. Trees must be sprayed to protect them against insects and fungi. "In Washington," Charles said, "they have to spray their trees ten or twelve times a year. We're higher and dryer here, so we only have to spray about half as much. Cooler days bring fewer bugs."

The fertilizer program that begins in May and June is "altogether different than for any other crop," Charles told me. "We use a calcium nitrate fertilizer, which has a neutral pH. Ammonium nitrate [commonly used on grain, for example] acidifies the soil. Calcium-deficient apples don't store as well. Orchard soils tend to be short on zinc and boron, so these are sprayed onto the leaves at intervals during the growing season."

I asked Charles about Alar, the now-banned substance formerly added to apples. "We didn't use it here. It was used primarily on Macintosh and Red Delicious apples as a growth regulator and color enhancer. It also kept the fruit a little more firm. We don't need it in Montana because of the triggering effect of warm days and frosty nights. These are ideal conditions to produce firm juicy fruit with good color."

Trees are planted about 20 feet apart. In the space between trees, a cover crop of ryegrass and white Dutch clover is planted. The approximate 20-foot spacing results in an average of 136 trees per acre in one of the Swanson's newer orchards, and 108 in the other. In places with milder climates, such as Washington, orchards often have 500 to 600 trees to the acre, Charles said. The difference is that trees in other areas are grafted on dwarf rootstocks, which cannot withstand the Montana climate. He pointed out that air is usually colder close to the ground, and the closer a tree is to the ground, the more vulnerable it is to cold snaps.

Starting usually around the end of the first week in September, the Swansons battle frost for their crop. Each of their newer orchards is equipped to fend off a few degrees of frost and keep the apples safe until harvest.

One of these frost-fighter devices is a 12-foot propeller atop a mast in the middle of the orchard. This propeller is powered by a motor that turns it at 500 r.p.m. During a temperature inversion, temperatures drop at the ground surface but remain warmer some distance above the surface. Typically, Charles said, temperatures may be 25 degrees at ground level, and 32 degrees at 50 feet above the ground. The propeller has an effective height of 50 to 60 feet, so warmer air from above can be brought down and kept down. As the propeller spins, it also rotates on the mast, at a rate of one turn per minute, to cover the entire orchard. Normally, Charles said, the propeller makes about a 50/50 mix of the colder air and warmer air, so the temperature in the orchard will be about halfway between the highest and lowest temperatures. If ground-level temperatures are 25 degrees and temperatures at 60 feet are 32 degrees, the orchard temperature will be about 27 or 28 degrees.

"Apples can stand sub-freezing temperatures as long as they don't get too cold or last too long. Most of our inversion frosts last three to five hours. We generally figure that apples can withstand twenty-six degrees for six hours, for example."

The other frost protection system is a sprinkler system, which protects the other newer orchard. This system generates what Charles called a "coarse mist." During the first stages of its operation, the mist coats everything it touches, including the trees, leaves, and apples, with a coat of ice. After that, the mist lands on the ice it has created and drips off. The laws of physics provide that as long as this dripping continues, the temperature of the ice crystals will never drop below 31.5 degrees. Charles said the sprinkler system must be turned before temperatures drop to less than 33 degrees, because it immediately reduces the temperature several degrees; from 33 to 26 or 27, for example. The wind machine also has to be turned on before temperatures get too low. Every system has its weakness, Charles said, and

ALAN & SANDY CAREY

Bitterroot Valley apples.

the problem with the sprinkler is that the sprinkler heads begin freezing up at about 21 or 22 degrees.

Frost protection is an absolute necessity, Charles said, adding that frost insurance is expensive and hard to come by. "Those insurance people will hold your feet to the fire if your orchard is at a high altitude in a cold area," he said, noting that his orchard is at 3,500 feet.

If the frost can be staved off, harvest usually comes in early October. The Macs are only in prime condition for about a week, so the Swansons hire 20 to 25 pickers to clear off the trees in this time. Macs can easily be damaged by too much finger pressure, so the pickers wear gloves to minimize damage.

DANIEL N. VICHOREK

Feeding the cider press at Swansons'.

Timing is tight in October, with the first killing frost, cold enough to ruin most or all the apples, usually coming about the middle of the month. The pickers work from ladders, and get paid 65 cents for each 40-pound box of apples they pick. "We have pickers who pick a hundred and twenty boxes a day, and others who pick thirty."

Charles said some pickers think his trees are too high, although they are pruned to about 15 or 16 feet, so as to be accessible from a 10-foot ladder.

After the apples are picked, they are stored in refrigerated facilities on the premises. Simultaneous with the picking, and continuing for as long as necessary afterward, apples are run through machines that polish them and sort them by size. Nothing is added to make the apples shiny, unlike the shiny waxed apples seen in the supermarkets. Sorted apples are placed in one-bushel, 40-pound cardboard boxes. Charles hauls these boxes to the stores where they are sold.

> There is hardly any variety of weather that cannot have some effect on apples.

All of the Swansons' apples normally are sold by Christmas. Elsewhere in the industry, apple sales extend over a much greater period. Technology is the reason a person can buy a fresh apple from a supermarket any time of year. Charles said that large producers join cooperatives that store their apples for long periods in specially equipped warehouses. These warehouses are filled with apples and the oxygen is drawn out and replaced with carbon dioxide. The temperature is then reduced to 32 degrees Fahrenheit. Apples stored under these conditions will stay firm for a long period, but storage costs boost the price about 10 cents a pound per month, Charles said.

I asked Charles if the apple business in the Bitterroot had the potential to expand and become more important. He said that the area's marginal weather will keep apple growing a small and undeveloped business. Besides the annual frost threat, trees can be damaged or killed by more extreme weather, such as the bitter cold snaps of 1988 and 1990. When I talked to Charles the next January, he was waiting to see whether his trees had sustained permanent damage in an autumn cold snap that froze the leaves before they could move their nutrient stores to the roots. "It got to two above zero before the trees were dormant," he said. Waiting to see how his investment survived the winter was nothing new.

There is hardly any variety of weather that cannot have some effect on apples. When I visited the Swansons during the last stages of their apple harvesting in October, their orchards were populated with numerous crews of local teenagers who were picking up apples that had been blown from the trees by a stout blast of wind. These were headed for the cider press. I bought three gallons of cider from the orchard of the original Charles Swanson. If anything better is made in Montana, I don't know what it is.

My editors at American Geographic mean well, God bless 'em, but sometimes they jump on a silly idea and ride off in all directions at once. For example, they told me with high confidence that nobody in Montana wants to be called a farmer. "Call 'em ranchers, or they'll get offended," one editor advised me.

"Well, okay," I said. "Tomorrow I'm going over to the Flathead to talk to a peppermint rancher. And I'll also be talking to an apple rancher in the Bitterroot."

As it turned out, neither Henry Ficken, the peppermint grower, nor Charles Swanson, the apple orchardist, wore a big hat or pointy-toed boots to indicate that they were ranchers. They seemed perfectly happy to be farmers. So much for good advice.

"I've been growing mint for twenty-three years right here. I'm a third-generation farmer," Henry Ficken told me on his farm south of Kalispell. "I used to grow lentils and peas and alfalfa, but now I grow mint and grain." Henry and his two sons, Mark and John, keep about one third of their farm in mint at any given time, in rotation with wheat and barley. Mint is a perennial crop, which, once planted, can be harvested every year for four or five years. The mint is then replaced with grain for four or five years. Rotating with grain helps break the cycles of weed and insect pests that can build up in the years when mint is grown. The soil is left undisturbed while mint is in the field, which makes it easier for plant and animal pests to get a foothold.

The mint crop grows from roots that can be planted either in the fall or in the spring. Planting is done with a special machine that makes four-inch-wide rows 22 inches apart. The mint planter has a conveyor on the floor that moves the roots forward to where the teeth on a spinning drum grab them and dump them into chutes. Shovels ahead of these chutes dig trenches the roots fall into, and a second set of shovels covers the roots.

Up through 1991, the Fickens obtained their roots from a grower in Idaho, but verticillium wilt was found at the source of these roots in 1991. Idaho roots are now quarantined and cannot be imported to Montana. Henry said Montana enforces this quarantine strictly, and that no roots can be brought into the state until they are certified verticillium free. "Verticillium wilt probably is the most devastating problem in the mint industry today," Henry said. Some of the mint growers in the Kalispell area raise mint for roots, so the Fickens and other growers can obtain roots locally.

Henry is recognized as a pioneer among mint growers in the Flathead. This year, he said, 22 or 23 farmers grew mint totaling at least 5,000 acres in Flathead County. Seven distilleries operate in the county to extract mint oil from the plants. The Fickens own and operate one of these stills.

Henry predicts that, in the future, more farmers will be growing mint. "Mint prices are better than grain prices. Specialty crops are your best bet for getting onto the profit side of the ledger."

Henry said that in his years as a mint farmer, he has seen the price of mint oil vary from $2.50 per pound to $25.00. In recent years, it has run in the $12 to $15 range. A pint of oil weighs one pound.

"Twelve dollars a pound sounds like a lot of money," Henry said, "but you've got to remember that mint is costly to raise."

One major expense is herbicides, which cost up to $400 per gallon, and don't always work. Where feasible, Henry said, herbicides are applied to individual plants, rather than broadcast.

Insecticides are another expense. Fifteen different insect pests attack mint plants, and each of them has to be suppressed. The Montana Mint Growers organization hires scouts to check each member's mint fields for insects each week. Most Montana mint growers belong to this organization, Henry said, calling it "the envy of the nation's mint industry." Insecticide use is minimized by keeping tabs on problem insect populations and spraying at the optimum times. Mint also requires very high amounts of nitrogen fertilizer, Henry said.

Another unusual aspect of growing mint as compared to most other crops is the prodigious thirst of mint plants, which, on the Ficken farm, require three inches of water per week. "This is intense water management," Henry said. "We irrigate regularly and constantly from the end of May until harvest." Water for irrigation is pumped from a slough on the

Mint harvesting on the Ficken place.

DANIEL N. VICHOREK

Henry, Mark, and John Ficken
MINT AS A FORM OF INSANITY

Ficken farm. I asked what sort of sprinkler system they use, and Henry told me they did most of their irrigating with a center pivot system and side-roll wheel-lines, but still were operating one hand-moved line, "that we like the way you like manual typewriters."

Harvest occurs in August and September, as the weather allows. "We cut it with a swather [machine for hay cutting] when about one tenth of the plants are in bloom. Then we

DIANE ENSIGN

Above: Near Whitefish.
Facing page: Flathead Lake barn.

The mint aroma is so strong, it'll almost knock you over.

let it wilt until it is slightly dry," Henry said. When the windrows are at the right stage of dryness, the Fickens use a regular hay chopper pulled behind a tractor to pulverize the mint plants. A water tank is mounted on the front of the tractor to spray the mint to increase its moisture, if necessary. The chopper blows the chopped mint into a special trailer pulled behind. During a September visit to the Ficken farm, the mint in the windrows was too damp

for optimum processing, but Henry and his sons took me out to the field and chopped a little to show me how it worked. When they had chopped a sample and blown it into the trailer, they urged me to climb up to the opening where the mint is blown in and check the mint aroma. "It's so strong, it'll almost knock you over," Henry said. "It'll just about knock you over," John said thoughtfully. "It will. It will knock you over," Mark said with conviction. So I climbed up and took a cautious whiff, and sure enough, it almost knocked me over.

The mint-hauling trailer has a single axle with dual wheels. When the trailer, referred to as a "tub," is full to its capacity of about six tons, it is unhooked and left standing in the field where a truck can hook up to it and pull it to the distillery at the Fickens farmstead where they extract the mint oil.

The power plant that runs the distilling process consists primarily of two oil-fired boilers that produce a total of 450 horsepower. Steam from the boilers is piped to each trailer full of chopped mint. Inside the trailer, steam at 15 pounds per square inch is distributed through a series of perforated pipes that lie about a foot apart and run full length on the floor of the trailer. Up to six trailers can be steamed at one time.

The trailers are sealed airtight, and the only escape for the steam and the vapor it drives out of the mint plants is through an outlet at the top. The vapors pass through this outlet at about 208 degrees Fahrenheit, and are piped into the still where the mint oil, which is as clear as water, is condensed and separated from the water vapor. About two hours is normally required to extract the oil from a trailer load. Steaming the annual harvest continues off and on over a period of about six weeks. The left-over plant material is dumped in the fields to be plowed back into the soil. After a few days these heaps of waste begin growing mold of such a vividly psychedelic coral-orange color that it looks like it ought to glow in the dark. I don't know if it does.

Following distillation, the oil is transferred into galvanized 55-gallon drums for shipping to wholesale purchasers. Henry said there are four major wholesalers of mint oil—two in Washington state, one in Indiana, and one in Michigan. These wholesalers sell the oil to manufacturers such as Proctor and Gamble, Colgate, and other companies that use it in toothpaste, gum, candy, medicine, and numerous other products.

I asked Henry what he and his sons do to keep themselves entertained during the winter. "Oh, we work in the shop," he said. It was clear that these shop projects were not just for fun. The Fickens welded and fabricated major portions of their still in their shop. John Ficken built one of the several trailers that they use to haul and process the mint, and everybody agrees it is better than the factory-made ones. Mark invented a device that makes coupling and uncoupling the trailers much quicker, "A big plus when we're on the tight schedule that goes with distilling."

"We used our heads and we learned how to weld," Henry said.

Regarding the profitability of growing mint, Henry said, "We're just starting to make enough to fix things up around here." When asked why anyone would want to be a farmer, Henry said, "It's just a form of insanity. Sort of a sickness that gets a hold of you."

I asked the Fickens how big a family farm like theirs has to be to support a family comfortably. They said that question is difficult to answer because of the large number of variables involved. However, they said that a farm that is debt free and raises a few high-dollar specialty crops has to be just about as big as a family can manage in order to make enough money for the family to get by. If land has to be purchased, they said, it is nearly impossible to pay for the land and support a family.

At present, they said, rural subdivisions in western Montana have inflated land prices to the point that even high-dollar specialty crops cannot compete against the land developers. "Big money people from out of state are moving in and paying prices for land that no local people can afford, displacing the very people who make western Montana what it is.

"Growing high-dollar specialty crops allows farmers more time to keep their farms as they get pressed by increased taxes and other costs associated with the influx of outside money. But I don't see any way that anybody could begin farming of any kind without outside help or income."

JEFF GNASS

Optimism may be more important than fertilizer and rain to Montana agriculture. Consider the viewpoint of Jon Clemenger, for example. Jon is a Christmas tree farmer near Kalispell. In the fall of 1991, there was much uproar over poor prices for Christmas trees, and major growers were tearing up their plantations and burning the trees.

Jon Clemenger took all this in, considered the situation, and said, "I'd say, now is the time to plant trees."

It's true, Jon said, that Christmas tree prices are down. "Prices are about the same as they were ten years ago, but down forty percent from what they were in the mid-Eighties." Of course, expenses have gone up and up in the last 10 years. Taxes have doubled, for example.

Under the present conditions, a tree grower needs business savvy and determination. In November 1991, Jon said he was expecting to sell up to 10,000 trees that year, more than in 1990, but for $2 per tree less. "You have to be more aggressive in this market," he said. The bulk of Jon's trees, about 80 percent, are Scotch pines, which normally wholesale for about $2 a foot.

About $2 of a tree's price is attributable to harvest costs, Jon said, noting that "raising Christmas trees is a labor-intensive operation."

"I substitute labor for land," he explained. "It's a way to make a living if you can only own a quarter section of land." Jon's 155-acre Christmas tree plantation has up to 25 workers at different times of the year, but mostly during harvest in November. Two or three people normally work for him during the winter.

Jon, a graduate forester and former employee of the U.S. Forest Service, has been planting trees since 1957. "I've planted more than a million trees," he said.

Planting a tree and harvesting a tree are not the same thing. Nationally, Jon said, three times as many trees are planted as harvested. The reasons for this disparity are not that much different than for any other crop. For example, a hailstorm in 1982 killed $75,000 worth of Jon's trees. In 1991, nature was kinder. Only about $25,000 worth of Jon's trees were killed, this time by meadow mice, one of the main pests to the Christmas tree farmer. Other problems include deer, which will eat spruce and fir in the winter.

"The deer spend the day sleeping on movie stars' lawns and at night they come over and eat my trees," Jon commented, alluding to nearby upscale residential developments.

The low winter sun also can damage trees by sunburning the bark. Insurance against such hazards is too expensive, Jon says, so he goes without.

The seven- to ten-year process of growing a Christmas tree on the Clemenger plantation starts with the planting of three-year-old seedlings in a barley stubble field. The stubble holds snow and protects the seedlings from wind erosion during their first year.

Planting is a three-person operation, normally done in March or April when the ground has thawed. One person drives a small tractor that pulls a furrow opener, which first opens and then closes a furrow. A second person rides the furrow opener and inserts seedlings into the furrow while it is open. The third person follows the furrow opener on foot and checks to make sure that the seedlings are spaced six feet apart, planted vertically, and otherwise OK. This person usually carries a few seedlings to replace others that are damaged or missing.

Jon said he normally plants about 10 percent of his acreage every year, to replace the 10 percent or so that he harvests. Planting usually is about 80 percent successful, Jon said, with about 20 percent of the seedlings dying because of lack of moisture or other problems. A replant is done the second year to replace the seedlings that don't make it. For the seedlings that don't make it after the second year, Jon said, "We just get used to the holes."

By the time planting is over, spring is moving along and with it the growth of weeds in the plantation. Jon's crew fights weeds with a four-foot-wide cultivator pulled behind a small tractor, and herbicides. Jon said it is important to select herbicides that will have the lowest possible impact on the environment while still doing the job.

After planting is finished, Jon goes to a commercial nursery and selects the year-old seedlings that he will grow in a plot by his house for two years before removing them for transplant into the plantation proper.

By early June, warm humid weather brings out the tree-eating bugs, such as aphids and western pine shoot moth, and a fungus disease known as "needle cast" which also

Below: *Jon Clemenger, at right.*
Facing page: *Flathead Valley hayrolls.*

DANIEL N. VICHOREK

Jon Clemenger
CHRISTMAS YEAR-AROUND

affects trees. These pests are controlled in part by removing the lowest branches from the trees to let air circulate, and by application of pesticides and fungicides. Any spare time during the growing season can be put to use trapping pocket gophers, which can do serious damage to growing trees.

Starting about the first of July and extending into August, the main chore around the Clemenger plantation is trimming the growing trees to the pyramid shape favored by Christmas tree buyers. Trimming is done with razor sharp, 16-inch knives designed especially for the purpose. Jon hires several people, often high school kids, to trim his Scotch pines. These workers are required to wear protective gear, including shin protectors of the type worn by baseball catchers.

DANIEL N. VICHOREK

Above: Jon Clemenger.
Facing page: Near Bigfork.

Once the summer trimming is over, it's time to "Fish for a few salmon and maybe cultivate a few weeds," Jon said. If the summer is abnormally dry, some irrigation may be done in August, using a handline sprinkler system.

Then in September, it's time to paint the Scotch pines. Jon said a coat of thin latex paint is applied to the trees to keep them green. Basically, Jon explained, this paint functions more as a suntan lotion than as a colorant. In the fall, he explained, some Scotch pines react to the shorter cooler days by withdrawing chlorophyll from their needles. Carotene that is left behind in the needles then makes the tree look yellowish. The paint keeps the trees from sensing the changing conditions, and as a result the chlorophyll remains in place.

October is the month for getting harvest equipment into shape, and then about November 1, harvest starts. Trees are harvested in November, Jon said, because December normally is too cold. At temperatures less than 25 degrees, the needles are brittle and trees are easily damaged by handling.

During my November visit to the Clemenger plantation, the tree harvest was in full swing. Trees are cut with gasoline-powered brush cutters that are slightly modified for cutting Christmas trees. These machines turn a carbide-tipped 12-inch circular blade at 10,000 revolutions per minute. The workers who do the cutting work in two-person teams. One of these workers is equipped with a 4x4 timber about eight feet long that is used to hold the low branches out of the way of the blade. The other person on the team operates the cutter. With one worker holding the branches out of the way, the operator of the cutter lowers the cutter blade next to the trunk until a skid under the blade rests on the ground. This places the blade about two inches above the ground surface. The cutting is accomplished with a quick thrust, and the four- or five-inch trunk is cut through in maybe a tenth of a second.

Once the trees are down, a worker with a chain saw cuts off the lowest branches and dresses the trunk if necessary so it will fit into a Christmas tree stand. Up to this point, trees of all species are treated the same. After the butts are trimmed, however, Scotch pines require an additional step that is not necessary for other species. This step is "shaking," which is accomplished on a special machine that gives the trees a brisk agitation to get rid of the loose dead needles that are characteristic of Scotch pine, which normally sheds needles more than two years old.

The final step in preparing Christmas trees for shipping is "baling." Baling is accomplished by running each tree through a baler that binds the branches tightly to the trunk with a spiral wrapping of twine. This reduces the shipping volume of the tree by about 80 percent. The baled trees are piled in rows so that a semi-truck can pull alongside for easy loading. At the Clemenger plantation, loading is performed with a bale elevator, a conveyor device normally used to stack small rectangular hay bales. Workers place the trees individually on the elevator, butt upward, and other workers on top of the load place them so the maximum number can be loaded. A semi-trailer normally can haul about 900 trees.

Following the harvest, there is a passel of accumulated paperwork—bills to pay, worker's compensation and Social Security withholding to be calculated and paid, and so on. This is also the time of cleanup, burning branches and other leftovers and waste.

Then in the deep snow of January, it's time to trim the spruces and firs to shape and size. This winter work is sometimes performed on snowshoes. Winter also is the time to fertilize trees—half a cup of granular fertilizer is placed on the snow at the base of each tree. And soon it is spring and time to start all over.

Most growers of other types of agricultural products might be intimidated by the seven- to ten-year period between planting and harvest of Christmas trees—a time during which there is no guarantee whether a fickle public may decide it doesn't need your product, or a surplus may develop and drop prices, or many another disaster might come along to bring ruin.

One need not look far to find threats to the Christmas tree business. How about the increasingly popular plastic Christmas trees, for example? Jon admitted that artificial trees have made some inroads into the market, but he believes that most people still want a high-quality natural product more than they want the convenience of a plastic tree. He said that a natural Christmas tree is a tradition, like a turkey for Thanksgiving dinner. "You don't see any synthetic turkeys," he said. Another selling point is that real Christmas trees benefit the environment, while a plastic tree is just another form of petroleum. Real trees protect watersheds, provide habitat for wildlife, and keep productive land from going into residential subdivision, besides providing oxygen to the atmosphere and absorbing carbon dioxide. When Jon gave me a tour of his plantation, I saw many deer tracks among the trees, and we saw a big cock pheasant hot-footing it down the rows. Overhead, sparrow hawks were hovering, waiting their chance at the endless supply of rodents that plague Christmas tree growers.

One impediment to Jon's business is the declining interest in Scotch pine for Christmas trees. Many tree buyers are coming to prefer other species, such as Fraser fir, which don't grow well in Montana. Jon said quality is usually more important than species. Growing conditions in Montana are perfect for Scotch pine, he said. "It takes a couple of good hard frosts to set the needles on Douglas fir and blue spruce, and once they are set, we can ship those trees to any point from Saskatoon to Texas and they won't lose many needles." Every state has Christmas tree plantations, Jon said, but Scotch pines grown in Montana are among the best there are, partly because of the climate. Climate is one of the things that makes Christmas tree growing a natural thing to do in the Flathead Valley. The Kalispell area has long been known for its Christmas trees. Jon pointed out that at one time, the area shipped 50 railroad cars of trees each year.

During my visit on the day before Thanksgiving, 1991, Jon and a dozen or so of his employees were busy loading Scotch pine on a truck that was going to haul them to a town near Banff in Alberta. The purchaser of the trees, Guy Sinotte, said he appreciates the quality of Montana trees. "One year I bought some Scotch pine from Ontario," he said. "I got a good deal on them, but when they were

delivered I discovered the dead needles hadn't been shaken out. I had to manually shake big gobs of needles out of each tree."

Sinotte said the quality of Scotch pines from Montana is in marked contrast to that of Scotch pines he has seen from other places—British Columbia, for example. Because of the warmer climate, he said, the B.C. pines "last about two days before their needles fall off." Sinotte said Canadians are not likely to lose their preference for Montana Scotch pines in the near future. "We're glad to get them," he said. Jon

Growing conditions in Montana are perfect for Scotch pine.

stated that a Scotch pine from Montana will retain its needles for about 30 days from the time it is brought into the house and set up.

This quality in Montana trees is part of the basis for Jon's optimism about the business. "People will always buy a quality product," he said.

I asked Jon how a Christmas tree grower supports himself between the first year of planting and the first year of harvesting. "Oh, you gotta have another job," he said.

JOHN REDDY

Above: Day's tree farm below the Swan Range near Ferndale.
Facing page: Hilger-area grain elevator.

"During those years, you work sixteen- and eighteen-hour days."

Besides growing trees for the wholesale market, Jon also operates a "choose and cut" operation for local people who want to cut a tree for themselves. Jon said that up to 200 hundred families come to his plantation to pick out a tree for themselves each year. Jon's observation of the tree selection process has led him to formulate "Murphy's Law of Christmas Tree Cutting."

Part one of Murphy's Law of Christmas Tree Cutting is: "People always take the first tree that they like, but they have to look at all the other ones first." Part two is: "The time taken to select a tree is inversely proportional to the temperature." If it's 40 above, it may take hours. If it's 20 below, it probably won't take more than two minutes. Number three is: "The time required to select a tree is inversely proportional to the number of people involved. If Pop shows up alone, he can probably find a suitable tree in five minutes. If Mom comes too, the time will extend at least a half hour. If there are kids with opinions, one day may not be enough."

Jon commented on the happy tradition of a family selecting its own tree giving rise to friction. To avoid this problem, Jon has advice for husbands: Let your wife pick the tree. The problem is, Jon said, that husbands and wives come from different family traditions regarding what constitutes a perfect Christmas tree. "You take a wife from New Jersey and a husband from eastern Montana and they're never going to agree."

But of course, Jon said, "Any tree looks good when you get your own decorations on it."

But what about the future? Will the Clemenger plantation be growing Christmas trees 20 years from now? The jury is still out on that one. The Clemengers have a grown son and daughter, and a daughter still in high school, and none of them seems inclined to get into the tree farming business. "One thing about farming anything," Jon said, "is that you tend to burn your kids out on it." Jon said that although both he and his wife Barbara (who works as a teacher) like to make a living growing things in the countryside, their children seem to prefer the big city lifestyle.

So what's going to happen to the land? "This place is my IRA [Individual Retirement Account]," Jon said. "All I have to retire on is what I can get from this place. I'd like to see it keep growing trees, but if it's worth more to subdivide, well, a lot of this land around here is being subdivided." He noted that nearby subdivided land goes for about $3,000 per acre.

GEORGE WUERTHNER

I'm probably a little bit different than the average rancher that has graduated from high school here and stayed here his whole life," Jim Peterson told me on his ranch at Buffalo, near Lewistown.

Jim did grow up nearby, following his father and grandfather who operated the family ranch, but he had to go out of state and spend 15 years as a financier before he could come back to live in Montana. "It's a good place to live if you can afford it," he said.

Jim has a Master's Degree in Business Administration, with emphasis in finance. Before he returned to Montana he was involved in corporate finance and cattle feeding in Texas and the Southwest. He said his education and experience give him a good perspective on the ranching business. "It's much more a business now than it used to be," he said. Jim uses a computer on his ranch to do his accounting, and he checks his finances every month. "You have to know what you can and can't do. You have to have some equity, you have to operate more efficiently than ranches used to run, and you have to keep tabs on your costs. Otherwise...well, the guy that had this place before I got it was a super good farmer. He expanded too fast, bought too much land, and he lost it."

Jim said it doesn't hurt to have a salary in the family from outside the ranch, to tide over the rough spots. He fills this requirement with his job as Executive Vice President of the Montana Stockgrowers, a job that takes him to his office in Helena three or four days a week.

Despite this absence, Jim said he oversees the day-to-day operation of the ranch. The ranch is a cow-calf operation that also grows wheat, barley, and alfalfa. Jim raises cross-bred calves, with black Angus cows and Simmental bulls. "My years in the feedlot business convinced me this was an excellent hybrid. The cows are good mothers, and the calves have a good hybrid vigor."

Jim's job with the Stockgrowers keeps him close to the issues affecting farmers and ranchers in Montana. "Our biggest challenge is to maintain traditional values. Easterners come out here and see this state and they say, 'We must preserve and protect this land for the future.' They tell their Congressmen, 'Do whatever you have to, but protect this land. Including from the people who live here.' So what we have here is a communication problem."

This communication problem, Jim said, results partly from the myth of the West. He cited the motion picture *Dances with Wolves* as an example of the western myth still in the making. "The myth is that the West has been ruined. In fact, the West is in the best shape now that it's ever been in. Read the journals of the pioneers and you see that there was cactus everywhere, and many of the rivers and streams were muddy and murky. Today the battle is between the preservation option, which would try to keep everything the way it is, or take it back to the way it is imagined to have been a hundred years ago, and the more traditional multi-use with economic reality, which we favor.

"In the last fifteen years we have endured a blizzard of legislation not friendly to agriculture. We have the National Environmental Policy Act, the Montana Environmental Policy Act, the Endangered Species Act, and the regulations on wetlands...just to name a few. And the new amendments to the Clean Water Act go way too far in regulating agriculture. All of these have tremendous implications for agriculture in the West. There is a tremendous concern and some over-reaction in favor of protecting resources. We say, resource protection must have an economic balance.

"People forget what made this country great, which is our ability to produce food and fiber. We produce the most abundant, cheapest, safest food in the world, and we have done it without damaging the environment. Look around at other places in the world if you don't believe it.

"People should realize that agricultural resources are renewable, and that preservation efforts have to consider economics. The Endangered Species Act, for example, is based solely on biological criteria, with no consideration

Below: Jim Peterson.
Facing page: *Winter feeding.*

DANIEL N. VICHOREK

Jim Peterson
THIRD GENERATION ON THE LAND

of the costs of protecting endangered species. Wetlands preservation is another thing that ignores economics. We feel that some revision is needed as regards what constitutes a wetland. They should be wet, for one thing. A lot of wetlands that exist today were actually created by farmers.

"So far, agriculture has been generally silent as more and more legislation has been passed that is not in our favor. Now, we have to be more outspoken. Besides being hard-working producers, we have to get more involved in telling our story."

This effort at resolving the communication problem between agriculture and the rest of the world promises to be an uphill struggle. "Today in the U.S., two percent of the people are involved in agriculture. A hundred years ago, eighty percent were involved in agriculture. Today's young people are a generation or two removed from the land. This gives them a different perspective on bread, eggs, milk, and animals.

"Our ability to govern ourselves as a state is going to be challenged by more populous states that want to save Montana for their posterity. California has fifty-four Congressmen. Montana has one."

In his role with the Stockgrowers, Jim lobbies the Montana legislature and the U.S. Congress in support of agriculture.

A major part of his efforts focus on proposed revisions to the Endangered Species Act, which he sees as a land use issue. Under the act, he said, wolves will be used to control land use. "Canada has fifty thousand wolves. We don't need 'em here," he said.

"People forget what made this country great, which is our ability to produce food and fiber. We produce the most abundant, cheapest, safest food in the world, and we have done it without damaging the environment."

JOHN REDDY

GEORGE WUERTHNER

Curtis Phipps is 57 years old and he lives at the very edge of the Missouri Breaks, 40 miles northwest of Jordan. His grandfather, R.N. Phipps, came to the country with an ox team in 1907, so the Phipps roots in those parts go deep. Curtis was born about 10 miles down the road from where he lives today. The Phipps farm and ranch is operated as a family corporation by Curtis and three of his brothers.

I went to the Phipps ranch because I was looking for isolation. I wanted to find out if there were truly isolated farmers and ranchers in Montana, and if so, what their lives might be like.

"I suppose I miss a few things," Curtis said, "but most of what I miss is to my benefit. Of course, my favorite pastime is to get on a horse and do a little riding." There is no television in the Phipps house. "We didn't have it before satellite dishes were available, and we didn't figure we needed it afterwards," Curtis said.

Curtis has 11 children. One of his eight sons, Kyle, an accounting student at Eastern Montana College, appeared, and I asked him if he remembered ever wanting a television when he lived at home. "Nah, we didn't have time. Dad made us cut wood."

"Yeah, these kids cut firewood to sell in Jordan to make themselves some spending money," Curtis said.

I asked Kyle if he had found out about anything that he had missed that he hadn't known existed, now that he was in college in the big city. He said he hadn't. Kyle went to the country school just down the road from the family ranch, and rode the bus 40 miles to Jordan every day to high school. He was valedictorian of his high school class. Kyle said Jordan High School has about 85 students. Curtis said the school in Jordan does not have the problem keeping faculty that some remote schools do. Kyle said his grade school and high school years prepared him well for the academic demands of college. Curtis pointed out that the smaller schools often do remarkably well not only in sports, but in more academic things such as spelling bees.

I asked Kyle where he intended to work after he is graduated. "Someplace in Montana," he said.

Curtis agreed with me that his ranch is isolated, but said he doesn't feel isolated. "We go into town to church every Sunday, and usually make one other trip to town sometime during the week. If somebody needs to go to the doctor we go to Miles City or Billings, and with good roads that doesn't seem very far."

I asked Curtis to fill me in on the annual routine on his ranch.

"Well,...starting about November, we start feeding cattle a little hay and cake [feed pellets]. The cake we have made out of our own barley in Jordan. Feeding cattle is what mainly keeps us busy all winter through April. I feed up to two hundred bales a day with a flatbed pickup. We do our calving in April. The cows have their calves out in the pasture. In April we also plant our spring wheat and barley. We used to grow some winter wheat but we had a bad year with it, and kind of got out of the habit. It takes about a week to do the planting.

"Then in May we do some fence fixing and start some field work, such as summer fallowing. We brand the calves early in June. We don't use a squeeze chute or any of that modern technology. We just get kids to wrassle 'em. We've got plenty of kids. Last time we branded, there must have been fifty kids there, but most of them were hoping to be just sightseers. We used to brand a little later, but the kids started complaining about the calves getting too big.

"All our hay is dryland grass hay, and we normally start cutting that in late June and run into July. When haying is over, or if we get held up by rain, we work on the combines to get them ready. Only one of our combines is a big one, so it usually takes us thirty working days to finish harvest. That goes from latter July to latter August. Then it's time to go to the Labor Day fair and rodeo in Jordan. In September, in between the odd jobs, we might do a little fishing. Go down to the reservoir and catch a few sand pike and walleye. Then in October or November, we ship our calves, and head right into the winter feeding cycle."

When I visited Curtis on the week before Christmas, he appeared to be somewhat at loose ends. The famous eastern Montana winter was nowhere to be seen. There was no trace of snow and temperatures were in the 50s. "It's been

Below: Curtis Phipps.
Facing page: Near Cardwell.

DANIEL N. VICHOREK

Curtis Phipps
CATTLE IN THE MISSOURI BREAKS

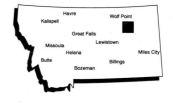

"A guy just has to hang in there."

an unusual year," Curtis said. "For example, we started out with thirty inches of rain [compared to the average 13]. Up on my neighbors' place where he's got grass growing on CRP, the grass is so tall that deer just disappear into it. Now we're not having much of a winter so far." We went out and fed a bucket of cake to his cattle so I could take pictures.

We talked about how things have changed around his

ALAN & SANDY CAREY

Above: Hunter at sunset. Facing page: Calf-branding roundup at Sula.

third the people here that were here 30 years ago. Some of them retired. A lot of them went under financially, mostly because they overspent."

Curtis wiped his forehead. "I should talk," he said. "Here not long ago we bought a neighbor's place and overextended ourselves. High cattle prices were all that saved us."

Methods of selling cattle have changed, Curtis observed. "We used to haul all our cattle to the sale barn in Billings or Miles City. Now we sell our calves under contract early in the year, and then in the fall we haul them into Jordan and weigh them, and the buyer takes them from there."

Hi-tech is also affecting cattle sales. Curtis explained how some of his neighbors have participated in a program that sells cattle with video. "They come and take video pictures of your cattle and then show the tape to buyers who bid. You have to stay by the phone while this goes on to accept or reject the bids." The video pictures are sometimes sent to faraway buyers through satellite transmissions.

One of the unusual things about the Phipps operation is their all-terrain cow pasture. Simply stated, they graze their cattle in the rugged breaks thereabout. Portions of this area are the closest thing Montana has to the Grand Canyon. "Yep," Curtis said with a small grin. "Last spring we turned two hundred and forty-two head of yearlings out there, and this fall we got every one of them back in good shape." The Phipps cattle are black Angus and Angus Hereford crosses. "The feeders want 'em, so we raise 'em."

I sat on the brink of the chasm leading down into the breaks and looked a mile or two into the rugged topography that is quite beautiful in a multi-hued gumbo sort of way. Far away and far below was a pale green puddle that is the remainder of Fort Peck Reservoir at this point. For some reason I was inspired to ponder the philosophy of vegetarianism. One argument for being a vegetarian is that cattle eat food that could be eaten by people. Although some of my favorite people are vegetarians, I could not visualize them hanging on by their

part of the country in his lifetime. "I remember when we used horses to farm," he said. "Then we used small tractors, and then we used bigger tractors. Along with this our outfit got bigger because we bought out several of our neighbors. People have been pulling out of here. There's less than a

toenails and munching the grass from those precipitous sidehills that made the Phipps cattle fat.

Curtis mentioned that his ranch is a good place to raise a family. "There's nothing bad going on around this neighborhood," he said. His children that have left home are "scattered all over the country," he said. One of his sons is the sheriff of Garfield County, of which Jordan is the county seat. Another is trying to get into ranching, but is having trouble. "We've got one hundred of his cows here on shares. He's tried everything to lease some land, but every time he finds a place, somebody else shows up with more money. It's just too tough to get started today."

Another problem is the possible loss of grazing on public land. "I guess that's what the environmentalists want," he said. The Charles M. Russell Wildlife Refuge comes right up to the Phipps place, and livestock is being forced off that land, Curtis said, adding, "I don't think old Charlie would think much of that idea."

Curtis is not much of a believer in government farm programs. "I've never bought into any of it," he said. "Not even federal crop insurance. We've never been hailed out up here, but one of my neighbors to the south had a hail loss that ran from fifty to one hundred percent this year.

"We'd all be better off if there were no government program. It's kind of a welfare program. People get dependent on it."

Government programs are not always easy to avoid, though. Curtis told me how he planted a crop of grass for his neighbor on land that his neighbor was putting into CRP, with the agreement that the Phipps would get part of the CRP money. The government found out about this arrangement and informed the Phipps that they were then included in the program. "What that means is, if you want to tear up some sagebrush and plant something, the government has to give you permission."

I concluded that it is harder to be isolated in Montana than it used to be. I didn't identify much in the way of disadvantages of being located way out yonder, and there were trade-offs even for these. "We don't get bothered much out here," Curtis said. "Not many salesmen. And we like it out here. It's home."

As for the future—"Well," Curtis said, "a guy just has to hang in there."

BRUCE HANDS

91

"When you write about me, be sure to tell the part about the monopoly," Gilles Stockton said at the end of our interview. Gilles, who operates a small sheep and cattle ranch just outside Grass Range, repeatedly made the point that the worst problem facing family-scale agriculture today is the agribusiness monopoly. "The sheep monopoly is going to be the demise of a lot of sheep growers," he said. "I've heard that producers who only have sheep have trouble getting financing because they don't have any cash flow. No banker can know when profitability will be reestablished."

Gilles said that monopolistic forces are only the most serious of the problems facing producers like him. "Besides that, we have urban and recreational interests moving in on what we like to think of as our prerogatives. We have the curtailment or elimination of grazing on public land, protection of wetlands. We have coyotes now, and we may have wolves later. The federal government promotes corporate agribusiness at the expense of small operators. There is an idea that we can import our food, and use our own land to raise deer, grouse, or buffalo. The idea of 'free trade,' removing controls on imported food, is death to us."

The idea that cattle are bad for the land is another problem that ranchers have. "Somebody, somewhere, decided that putting cattle on rangeland is damaging. Anybody with eyes can see that's not true. Rangelands may be in better shape now than in the buffalo days. In those days, buffalo didn't get too far from water, and land near the water got trampled. I've seen the same thing with wild game in Africa.

"All this controversy, this 'Cattle Free by '93' [slogan of Earth First!, a radical environmental group], is extremely painful to ranchers. You couldn't hurt them more. They are being told that everything they believed in, their life's work, is worth nothing, and is destructive.

"This is a culture that doesn't know the value of food. A lot of Americans hate us and envy us and are ignorant of what it takes to produce food. City people don't care about us. You can read the Billings *Gazette* for a year and not know there is a cow in Montana. People in Great Falls and Billings don't care about us, and people in the other towns *sure* don't care about us. We don't have any clout because we are losing our population."

Gilles said he recently was talking to some urban types who quite smugly pointed out that farmers resist going to no-till farming, as though this was a sure indication of farmers' irresponsibility. "I told them, 'You want to know

what no-till farming is? It's farming with chemicals, using chemicals to do the work normally done by machinery. No farmer likes chemicals. Farmers use the fewest chemicals they can and still get by.' But this is an example of the sort of ideas people have about farmers.

"Urban environmentalists need to understand that they are not the inventors of conservation. Farmers and ranchers live within and manipulate nature to make their own living and produce food for others. Environmentalists are potentially our best ally, if they had a better understanding of how things work. The situation we are in right now polarizes the issue. Agricultural people are more and more vulnerable to manipulation by extreme far right politicians."

Gilles Stockton has deep roots in the Grass Range country. His grandfather surveyed the railroad right-of-way, which now runs, abandoned, through the family ranch founded by the grandfather. Gilles' father spent his life on the family ranch, where he is now retired. The elder Stockton is the author of the book *Today I Baled Some Hay to Feed the Sheep the Coyotes Eat,* a long-time favorite Montana book. Gilles lives in the town of Grass Range, which looks prosperous for that part of the country, and commutes three miles to his work on the ranch. I talked to him one evening in his kitchen in town, and went to visit the ranch the next day.

"I grew up here," Gilles said, looking at home in the yard at the ranch. After graduating from Grass Range High School, Gilles went to Rocky Mountain College where he studied biochemistry and French. "I was thinking of becoming a doctor," he said. After college, Gilles joined the Peace Corps

Below: Gilles Stockton.
Facing page: North of Wilsall.

DANIEL N. VICHOREK

Gilles Stockton
FAMILIES VERSUS AGRIBUSINESS

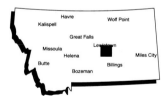

and went to Africa, where he did agricultural consulting. Later, back in the states, he did civil rights work in Mississippi, and eventually joined the Peace Corps staff in Washington, D.C. The Peace Corps assigned him to "a little green cubicle," in a big office building, and it wasn't long before he decided to return to Grass Range. "I came back in '75," he said. Before he came back for good he stopped off at Montana State University to study animal science.

DANIEL N. VICHOREK

Above: Toby the guard dog.
Facing page: Grain elevator at Grassrange.

These days, Gilles is busy raising sheep and cattle on the ranch. "We're about half sheep and half cows. You can use the land more intensively when you have both. Also, it spreads the cash flow out a little better. If you just have cattle, you only get paid once a year."

In order to get paid more than once a year, Gilles still takes consulting jobs with federal agencies, working to help

develop agriculture in Africa. He has worked with U.S. AID—a branch of the State Department—with the World Bank, and with Save the Children.

Back home, Gilles considers the state of agriculture here. "The next decade is going to be tough. Not only tough but tough tough. After that, it's anybody's guess. One thing I'm sure of: family farming and ranching is ecologically and economically the best use of this land. Look at the drought of the 1980s. It was as severe as the droughts of the 1880s and 1930s, but the impact on land and livestock was almost nonexistent. This was because we have improved the way we ranch. We have developed our water, spread our livestock around, and developed hay land.

"We are now in the third stage of Montana agriculture. The first stage was the huge cattle operations of the 1880s. They lasted, what, ten years before the weather did them in. The next stage was homesteading, which was wrong for the land, and also collapsed. Now we're in the third stage.

Third-stage agriculture includes feeding hay to the sheep the coyotes eat, and I rode along with Gilles while he did this. First, however, he introduced me to Toby, a Great Pyrenees dog. Toby's job is to make sure no coyotes eat any sheep. He is a guard dog. "We forgot about these dogs," Gilles said. "As a business we forgot about them. These were the Basque herders' dogs, and we forgot about them."

Gilles said guard dogs have been pretty effective in protecting against coyotes. "So far this year, we've only lost one lamb," he said. "One of our neighbors lost thirty-five, and another lost forty. The neighbor that lost thirty-five also had a dog, so these dogs are not foolproof. Sometimes they can be outsmarted by a coyote, or a pair of coyotes."

Most of the day, Toby lies around the ranch buildings, far from the sheep he is supposed to protect. "He doesn't work during the day, and that is one way they are not foolproof. But sometimes he'll smell something, maybe a coyote, and then he'll be up and headed over to check on his sheep. And in the evening, he goes to work and stays with them all night. If a coyote comes, he chases it off. He doesn't kill coyotes, and he doesn't think he's a sheep or anything like that.

"It's not the greatest situation having the dogs cross the county road to get to where the sheep are. We've lost dogs from being hit on the road." Toby, on the other hand, seems to be indestructible. "He's been hit by cars. Didn't hurt him. He got to chasing a neighbor's cattle, and the neighbor shot him twice with a twenty-two, once in the shoulder and once in the hip. Didn't hurt him."

We hauled a few bales of hay out to where the sheep were, and as we approached, the cab of the pickup made a crumpling sound above our heads as Toby got up on it. He kept going down onto the hood and off onto the ground in front of the pickup, and trotted off to join the sheep. Toby acted like he owns the sheep, approaching them in a familiar manner, looking at this one and that one, and then moving on. The sheep pay no attention whatsoever.

"They get used to the individual dog, not the breed. I got a new dog recently, same kind, same color, but the sheep ran away from her until they got used to her."

Back at the ranch buildings, Gilles admitted that although he has a certain pessimism about the state's agriculture, he also retains an element of optimism, which he said you have to have, along with patience, to operate in agriculture. "You have to be in it for the long haul. You have to be like the tortoise. One thing, though, if you are at all subject to depression, a ranch is not a good place to be. You work all by yourself with nobody to talk to most of the time. I think that's what causes the drinking. The ranch culture in general has a high alcoholism rate."

As we wound up our talk, Gilles reminded me again: "Monopoly is our worst enemy. Environmentalists we can fight politically, but we can't fight the monopoly."

I asked Gilles about the future of the family ranch. "Well, when our son gets out of high school, we might start taking some longer-term consulting contracts. There's always somebody who wants to lease a place, and we could come back whenever we wanted to." There's no way of knowing whether Gilles' son Antoine will ever want to run the ranch. Right now, it doesn't appear to appeal to him. Antoine no doubt will follow his father's example and head out into the larger world, but in case he winds up in a green cubicle somewhere, the ranch will be waiting for him. That, as I understand it, is the idea. ■

"Monopoly is our worst enemy. Environmentalists we can fight politically, but we can't fight the monopoly."

RICK JACKSON

95

ART WOLFE

Noreen Lehfeldt and her husband John live with their two children in a little house on the crest of a hill just outside Lavina. "It's always a dilemma," Noreen said, "whether to build on a hill where you can see something, or down in a coulee where you can be protected from the wind. We decided to build on the hill and superinsulate, so we could have the best of both worlds."

On the day I visited, a fine clear December day, the wind was on the keen side. "That's no chinook," Noreen said, noting the sharp edge on the gust. "Sure isn't," I said. And then we talked about chinooks, and what a fine thing it is to live in a country where there are chinooks. "In one of Ivan Doig's books, I think it was *Dancing at the Rascal Fair,* he told about chinooks," Noreen said. "I really liked the way he described the Scotchmen discovering the chinooks."

But regular wind is something else. "It'll drive you crazy around here," she declared.

Away from the Lehfeldt house a ways is a kennel that was full of border collies the day I was there. Noreen explained that she raises and trains the dogs to work sheep, and sells them. Noreen opened one cage and out popped Meg, a friendly female. We took Meg and got into the Lehfeldts' pickup to have a look around. First we went to a nearby feedlot which was bulging with fat lambs in the process of getting even fatter.

On the way over to the feedlot, I asked Noreen how long the Lehfeldts had been in the sheep business. She pointed at an imposing old barn next to the sheeplot and said, "See that barn? John's grandfather built it. Then he lost the place, and later on John's dad bought it back. They've been in the sheep business a long time."

In the barn, Noreen showed me an Australian-made machine that bales wool. Having always heard that one of the worst jobs on the planet was stomping wool into sacks, I was glad to hear that I was safe from it at last.

When we finished looking over the fat lambs, we got back in the pickup and headed north to look as some sheep out on the range. It became evident that there is a lot of range north of Lavina. We drove and drove, and saw no other vehicles or sign of settlement, except for the rare homestead artifact, such as an old school house.

"There's a lot less people around here than there used to be," Noreen said. She began pointing in different directions as she spoke. "Over that way there used to be an old couple, but they sold out. Up that way an old couple still

lives, but there's nobody to take over their place when they're gone. Off in this direction a ways is an old fellow who has his place up for sale, but he's asking way more than it's worth. He'll live there until he dies, and then I suppose we'll buy the place."

I asked about the famously low price of lambs, and the possible reason thereof. Noreen said she didn't know. "Right now, lambs are worth forty-eight cents a pound. A few years ago they were worth ninety cents. I noticed that all during this time, lamb stayed at seven ninety-nine in the supermarket. None of the butchers went broke when we were getting ninety cents, so something is out of whack somewhere. I hear people say that the government ought to step in, but I don't like to hear that."

Noreen told me that she and her husband recently went with an exchange program to Kazahkstan, a sheep-raising area in the former USSR. In Kazahkstan, she said, there is evidence of what the government can do in agriculture. She mentioned a collective farm they visited, which was required by the government to have 5,000 sheep. Drought had come, and the 5,000 sheep had devastated the land. "I never saw anything like it," she said.

Noreen said the differences between raising and marketing sheep in Montana and in Kazahkstan were so great that there was no common ground for communication. "We eventually just talked about families and such," she said. There also was some question about the reliability of their interpreter. "She asked me what we did with our lambs, and I said we sold them. She was appalled by this. She said we should give them to the government. Then we wondered what she was telling the others about us."

Having dealt with the drought and other matters in Kazahkstan, we were still headed north across no man's land, going up to look at sheep. Noreen was explaining the functioning of the Lehfeldt sheep operation. "Basically, we are in good financial shape," she said. "The reason for this is how smart the people are that run it: my husband, his brother, and their dad. We have way

Below: Noreen Lehfeldt.
Facing page: Montana winter field.

DANIEL N. VICHOREK

Noreen Lehfeldt
RANCHING ALLOWS FAMILIES TO BE IN BUSINESS TOGETHER

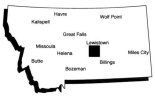

more animals than we have land for. We buy feed, pay someone so much to run our sheep out in a wheat stubblefield, for example. Or if somebody gets hailed out, we pay them to graze sheep in what's left. This is a good deal for everybody. It gives the owner of the pasture some money he wouldn't have got otherwise, and it gives us a place for the sheep.

"Another thing we have done is breed selectively for fine wool. Fine wool is what they use to make a woman's high fashion dress, or a good wool shirt. There is a limited amount of fine wool, and we get a better price for it."

After a while, the good gravel road turned into a dirt road. Then we left the dirt road and headed overland. A half mile away, there was a band of sheep. "When we get closer," Noreen said, "a guard dog will come out to meet us. That's what they do when something unusual happens." And sure enough, as we approached over the rough ground, the sheep ran into a tight flock and stayed there, and a large white dog came out to challenge us, barking.

"We have five guard dogs," Noreen told me. This one is a *maremma,* an Italian breed that looks a lot like a Great Pyrenees. "We selected them because they have the greatest success in training to be guard dogs, about eighty percent. Not every dog that you try to train can become a guard dog. The ones that don't make it as guard dogs aren't any good for anything else. They're not socialized to be pets, so you can't use them for that. Generally, you have to shoot the ones that can't be trained. We wanted to shoot as few as possible, so we chose these maremmas." Noreen raises one litter a year of guard dogs and sells any the ranch doesn't need.

We approached the sheep on foot, and the big white dog continued to advance toward us, not looking too friendly. Noreen called and called to her. Finally she approached us cautiously, greeted Noreen in a business-like manner, checked a bucket of dog food that Noreen had brought, and then headed back over to the sheep, a hundred yards or so away. Meg, the border collie, saw the sheep too, and was seized by her breeding and training. She was in a trance, eyes fixed firmly on the sheep, tail tucked under, head down. Her total existence was tuned to the imminent opportunity to herd sheep. If you could ask a border collie, "What is the meaning of life?" there could be only one answer: herding sheep.

When we got a bit closer, Noreen gave a command and Meg ran counterclockwise around the band of sheep.

"What does that command mean?" I asked.

"It means, run around the sheep counterclockwise."

The sheep were perfectly sheeplike, and the whole bunch quickly began rotating counterclockwise. Almost immediately the band formed into a perfectly round group. The big guard dog was nowhere in sight, but was compressed somewhere in the middle of the band. "Lay down," Noreen ordered, and Meg lay down. She was on the other side of the sheep from where we are.

We stood and looked at the sheep without speaking. Nothing was moving except the abundant grass that gyrated in the wind. It was 10 inches high and in the low December sun it was a fine spun-gold strawberry blonde color. It was more golden than any gold I have ever seen. We were in the middle of a lonely plain that seemed almost endless in every direction. We were very small in the precise center of it. From a satellite, I imagined, a small woolen disc would be visible in the middle of all this grass. We probably would not be visible ourselves, though possibly our long shadows could be seen.

To the north, the Big Snowy Mountains were big and snowy. To the west, visible from just over the ridge, the Crazy Mountains were huge, blue and white—their ruggedness indistinct in a local windstorm that was blowing the snow around. Mysterious, like Shangri-la.

Presently Noreen called Meg, and we headed back to the pickup, leaving behind a small bucket of food for the guard dog. The wind that had been sharp was now getting raw. We were glad to get into the pickup and head up the road once more.

"One of the things that intrigues me more and more about farming and ranching is the dynamics of families," Noreen said. "Outside of farming and ranching, not many families are in business together. It's interesting to watch what happens when families are in this situation. On our place, my husband is good with the livestock so he takes care of that end of it. His brother has good mechanical ability and likes to work with the machinery, so he does most of the farming. It works out fine for us. Other families are not so lucky."

Noreen was not brought up on a ranch. She was raised

DANIEL N. VICHOREK

Above: John Lehfeldt.
Facing page: Before the storm.

If you could ask a border collie, "What is the meaning of life?" there could be only one answer: herding sheep.

in Butte. I asked her if it was difficult making the adjustment from town to country.

"One thing that was hard was getting used to the idea that your life and your job are the same thing. When my dad came home from work, he was done for the day, and could do whatever he wanted. That's not the way it is in a ranch. There's always something else to do. Your job and your life are the same. Besides that, it gets too hot around here in the summer."

Having inspected the sheep, fed the dog, and photographed the whole scene, we proceeded north. We were headed to a set of corrals where Noreen's husband, John, was working cattle. We saw the corral some distance off with three roads running that general direction. We took the road on the right. No, that wasn't it. We went back and took the road on the left. Not it. We took the middle road, and soon arrived. Nobody was there, except a few forlorn cattle in a truck. Noreen deduced that her husband and the hired man had finished with the cattle and were driving them north. We took off in that direction. Pretty soon we found two winterized cowboys on shaggy ponies driving a couple hundred black cattle. We pulled alongside the riders. One of them got down and shook my hand. He said he was John Lehfeldt. He asked if I had enough information. I said I thought I did. He said the last time some writer came and interviewed his wife, the write-up said Noreen owned the whole ranch herself. "You mean she doesn't?" I said. It was getting to be late afternoon for that time of year, and the wind was getting colder.

John got back on his horse and headed north and we got back in the pickup and headed south. We were out of ranch-related topics for the moment, and we began talking about big cities, and how it is nice to visit there but not live there. "Moscow," Noreen said. "What a city. It stank and we almost starved to death, but it is a fine city."

In the long ride back I mentioned some of the problems other farmers and ranchers are having. "We don't have many problems," she said. "We don't have any movie stars moving in around here. Most people think this part of the state is ugly. We don't get many hunters. Eagles don't bother our sheep. We haven't had any predator problems at all since we got our guard dogs. Sure, the market's sluggish, but sooner or later, it has to bottom out and come back. It always has, and when it does, we'll be ready."

PATRICIA PRUITT

99

Clint Peck is editor of the *Montana Farmer-Stockman*, a monthly agricultural publication from Billings. I interviewed him to obtain a broad perspective on Montana agriculture.

"There is a misunderstanding," he said, "about farmers and ranchers and their care of the land. In our paper, I try to tell stories of farmers and ranchers as stewards of the land. In general, farmers and ranchers are extremely good stewards. Ninety percent of the land is well-taken care of, and we need to be proud of that. Everywhere I go in the state, I see examples of conservation and enhancement of resources.

"There are examples of poor stewardship, and these need to be taken care of. These poor examples are the glory of people who want to criticize agriculture. There are people with an agenda who want livestock removed from public land. One of the best known examples of livestock impacts on the land is in the upper Ruby River valley. In that area, one small area that is highly visible was trampled all to hell. Nobody talked about the rest of the drainage where there wasn't any problem. The Montana Wildlife Federation went to court, the Forest Service prepared an environmental impact statement, and now it looks like the Forest Service is going to recommend a 40 percent reduction in grazing in that area.

Clint said there is plenty of evidence that wildlife and cattle can exist together. One of the best examples is on the Wall Creek Game Range south of Ennis. There, cattle are pastured on elk winter range to improve the range for elk. Cattle like forage that is tough and woody, but elk like more palatable, succulent forage. Without cattle, there wasn't enough grazing pressure to keep the tougher forage grazed back. By the early 1980s, tough forage was keeping elk from using many areas of the game range.

When livestock grazing was reintroduced on an experimental basis, elk numbers quickly grew. Today, 694 cattle are allowed to graze the range, and elk numbers on the winter range have grown to 1,400. That's up from the 700 or so that were there in 1970. Everybody is happy

with this arrangement: sportsmen, fish and game employees, the Forest Service, and ranchers.

Clint cited another example of agriculture and wildlife existing in harmony. South of Malta, Willie Doll, operator of the Diamond Willow Ranch, has built 200 stock reservoirs, some of which he fenced and planted with trees and shrubs to provide cover and forage for wildlife. He has also installed nesting sites for ducks and geese. Doll keeps the fences closed on these enclosures during times of the year when cattle would trample eggs or young birds. Doll said, 'What's good for the wildlife is good for cattle.' A wildlife biologist working with Doll said that substantial numbers of pintails and mallards are being produced on the ranch. With his reservoirs and other strategies, Doll has nearly tripled his beef production without expanding his land base.

The grass ecosystems of the great plains evolved in response to grazing pressure, Clint pointed out. Some types of grass depend on trampling for reproductive success. "The northern great plains are specifically adapted to grazing. They can be managed to prevent damage and continue the ecological system."

Clint said the journals of pioneers gave good indications of what range conditions were before Europeans arrived. "Read the journals of Lewis and Clark. They talk about how barren the land was on their portage around Great Falls. Cactus every place. Today, we know that what is good for the land is good for the long-term productivity of the land."

I asked Clint about the loss of farm and ranch populations and the increasing size of agricultural units. "We made a serious mistake a long time ago," he said. "We had the idea that granddad's old hundred and sixty or three hundred twenty acre farm could support the whole family. The truth was, somebody was going to have to leave that farm. Over the years, more and more young people have left the farms, and these farms have been bought by other farmers. I believe that most of the shakeout has now occurred. We are real close to finding the stable population our farms and ranches can support. We have been moving in that direction for a hundred years. We in Montana are through our adolescence as farmers and ranchers dealing with our environment here. In the Midwest, they are ahead of us. They have been farming two hundred years in the Midwest, three hundred years on the east coast, a thousand years in Europe. We are just entering our early maturity as farm and ranch operators here. We know now that we have

DANIEL N. VICHOREK

Clint Peck
FARMERS & RANCHERS AS STEWARDS OF THE LAND

to deal with the drought cycle, long-term. Water resources are one of our chief limitations on agriculture.

"Our evolution toward sustainability has been warped by the war years. Prices go up in wartime, and farmers and ranchers have an easier time. Evolution also is affected by the technology factor. New types of grain that produce better in dry conditions, new irrigation technology, new livestock genetics, new farm machinery, are all part of the technology factor that increase productivity.

"Ranchers are learning to use the land they have more intensively, rather than acquiring more land." Clint pointed to the example of Jim Sindelar, who raises 200 cows on 150 acres along the Yellowstone River east of Billings. "Compare that to [pioneer cattleman] Granville Stuart, who ran cattle all over ten thousand sections." The main part of Sindelar's strategy is to rotate the cattle among a series of 10- to 15-acre pastures in the river bottom.

"There is a wrinkle or caveat in this evolution," Clint said. This wrinkle is the "encroachment of elitism." These elitists are "people who are drawn to Montana but don't need to live off the land. They look at things differently than people who have to make their living here. They bring different values with them. To some extent, we will have to conform to their way of life. In Paradise Valley, for example, farmers and ranchers will have to deal with the increased land values. The long-term effects of the elitist encroachment depend on whether it keeps spreading. The way to fight encroachment is to give the agricultural producers a better price for their products so they can afford to stay on the land."

Clint asserted that agriculture is a business much like any other business. "The same sort of decisions have to be made. The people on the farms and ranches face the same sort of challenges as the rest of us. For example, how many farm wives have jobs in town? Lots of them. How many farmers have a sideline selling farm chemicals for extra income? Lots of them. It's just like urban families in Billings: there are no single breadwinners in families anymore. Farmers and ranchers do need a wider range of skills than city people normally need. They have to be mechanics, veterinarians, bookkeepers, agronomists, plumbers, welders, and so on.

"One thing I've thought about a lot; I've asked myself this question over and over. Say you've got a corner grocery store that has been in the family for three generations. Then say a mall comes in nearby, and a supermarket, and times get tough. My question is, is it harder for that family

to sell that grocery store than it is for the rancher out at Roundup to sell his ranch when things get tough? I don't know. Some people say the attachment to the land makes it tougher for the rancher, but I don't know."

Clint foresees a lessening of environmental pressures on agriculture as time goes by. "Farms and ranches that have a sustainable size will bring increasing pride of ownership. Owners are going to be more and more careful about water, land, and noxious weeds. They are going to avoid taking more out of the soil than they put in. There's a lesson for us to learn in eastern Europe, where collective management has depleted the land.

"I'm also optimistic that some maturity is going to come into environmental consciousness. I see evidence that extreme environmentalists are being replaced by moderates. The wilderness people spent ten thousand dollars to put an ad in the New York *Times* soliciting funds. I hear they got four thousand. Now if they'd got four million, my ears would have perked up."

I asked Clint about the monopolistic forces often cited as affecting agriculture. "It's true," he said, "that there is a concentration of resources in the hands of a few in almost every segment of agriculture: grain, meat packing, oil seeds, fuel and fertilizer for some examples. But, is that any different from any other segment of society? There's a limited number of people that sell us our gasoline, for example." As regards the monopoly in beef packing, he said, it has been investigated several times and there was no proof that it was affecting prices of beef. However, the Justice Department is investigating possible anti-trust violations in the sheep industry.

"Ranchers are learning to use the land they have more intensively, rather than acquiring more land."

PAUL CONKLIN

Rural patriotism in Central Montana.

T. J. Gilles is agriculture editor for the Great Falls *Tribune*. Because of the nature of the interview, I have placed it in question and answer format.

Q. So what is the future of agriculture in Montana?

A. [Gives thumbs down.] West of the divide, there is no future. In Paradise Valley and along the mountains down to Red Lodge, there is no future. Those of us who grew up here need to realize that we are now in the place of the Indians and Eskimos.

Remember why our ancestors took the land from the Indians? We had a higher and better use for it. Now some new people have come to take the land from us. They had a higher and better use for it.

Q. The land grab of the rich and famous?

A. Yep. Of course that's not true east of the mountains. You don't see many movie stars on the plains. This was explained to me the other day in terms of distorted aesthetics. I hitched a ride with some folks from Conrad. They said distorted aesthetics was what keeps Conrad from being the Aspen of the plains. Perverted aesthetics is what makes people prefer snow-capped mountains and trees and clear running water to the wide open spaces of the prairie. How come, they said, everybody wants purple mountain majesties, and nobody wants amber waves of grain? So there you have it....You have to realize what happens when rich people come and pay a fortune for a place. The land values skyrocket, and then when the rancher next door dies his son has to pay five hundred thousand dollars inheritance tax on a place that was bought for two thousand dollars back in nineteen ten. He can't do it, so he sells out and maybe gets a job managing the place. Pretty soon, us locals will be limited to doing the cooking and fetching for the rich folks.

Q. So what happens to agriculture east of the mountains?

A. Who knows? Somewhere there are people thinking about the future of agriculture in Montana, although maybe they've never been here or heard of it. We don't know who they are or how they come up with their conclusions. They might say, "Why should we encourage people in Montana to try to grow crops? They hardly have any soil, and they all buy federal crop insurance and collect almost every year. We're lucky if they get through the year without collecting disaster payments. Why don't we cut off these Montana guys and put out incentives to California farmers to grow another crop each year instead?"

Or, they might say, "Those California farmers use too many chemicals and too much water. Let's cut them off and help out those Montana farmers. They only grow crops every other year and don't use a lot of chemicals up there and we like to encourage that." Who knows? We don't know who these people are or what they might do or when they might do it.

Q. Any other insights?

A. This gives me a chance to cite Gilles' principle of agricultural profit. Originally Kurths' principal. [Some members of the Kurth family were convicted of growing marijuana to pay off debts on their grain farm near Fort Benton.]

Q. And that is?

A. The farther something is from the basic needs of life, the more you can make growing it. Grow wheat and you get nothing for it. Grow a cow and you don't get much. Grow an ostrich and you get a fortune. Grow a llama and you make a pile. Grow tame elk that a dude can shoot out in the pasture without the inconvenience of getting up early and climbing steep mountains and you make a bundle. Grow exotic goats...but you get the picture.

Q. Anything else?

A. We need to maintain our distinction from rich people who come and buy our land.

Q. How do we do that?

A. Do it in small ways. I edited a news release for the Montana Weed Control Association. Their keynote speaker was Tom Brokaw. They wanted to call him, "a Montana landowner." I changed that to "An owner of land in Montana." That's subtle, but it's important. We don't want people to think he's one of us. In the end, Brokaw only appeared on videotape.

Below: *T.J. Gilles*
Facing page: *Near Polaris.*

DANIEL N. VICHOREK

T. J. Gilles
HOLDING LITTLE HOPE FOR THE FUTURE

103

INDEX